# THE AMERICAN REVOLUTION AND "A CANDID WORLD"

# The American Revolution and "A Candid World"

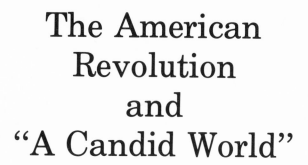

*edited by*
*LAWRENCE S. KAPLAN*

THE KENT STATE UNIVERSITY PRESS

ISBN: 0-87338-205-6
Library of Congress Catalog Card Number: 77-6671
Manufactured in the United States of America


**Library of Congress Cataloging in Publication Data**
Main entry under title:

The American Revolution and "A Candid World".

  Includes bibliographical references and index.
  1. United States—Foreign relations—Revolution, 1775-1783—Congresses. 2.
United States—Foreign relations—1783-1815—Congresses. I. Kaplan, Law-
rence S.
E249.A54       973.3'2       77-6671
ISBN 0-87338-205-6

When in the Course of human Events, it becomes necessary for one People to dissolve the Political Bands which have connected them with another, and to assume among the Powers of the Earth, the separate and equal Station to which the Laws of Nature and of Nature's God entitle them, a decent Respect to the Opinions of Mankind requires that they should declare the causes which impel them to the Separation.

. . . The History of the present King of Great-Britain is a History of repeated Injuries and Usurpations, all having in direct Object the Establishment of an absolute Tyranny over these States. To prove this, let Facts be submitted to a candid World.

IN CONGRESS, July 4, 1776
A DECLARATION
By the Representatives of the
UNITED STATES OF AMERICA,
In GENERAL CONGRESS assembled

# Contents

# PREFACE

This book grew out of a bicentennial conference held on May 14 and 15, 1976 at Kent State University by the Kent American Revolution Bicentennial Commission, the Department of History, and the Artist-Lecture Series of Kent State University, with the cooperation of the Division of Continuing Education of Kent State University and the Ohio American Revolution Bicentennial Advisory Commission, and with support from the George Gund Foundation of Cleveland. Donald M. Hassler, co-chairman of the Kent Bicentennial Commission, provided the link between town and gown that accounted for the success of this and other programs in 1975-76.

My colleague, William Howland Kenney, helped win respectability among colonial historians for this gathering of diplomatic historians. Through his agency the conference was designated as the 37th Conference in Early American History of the Institute of Early American History and Culture.

In addition to the scholars presenting and commenting on papers, the conference benefited from the presence of colonial historians Don R. Gerlach of the University of Akron and John Cary of Cleveland State University, who chaired panels on the "Anglo-

American Relationship" and "Other Parts of the World," respectively. I want to record a special debt to Warren F. Kuehl of the University of Akron who accepted a last-minute invitation to chair the session on "Franco-American Relations."

LSK

# INTRODUCTION

In the Declaration of Independence, the Founding Fathers presented to a "candid world" their justification for revolution. "A decent respect to the opinions of mankind" required that other nations witness and approve the actions of the British colonists in America. What the authors did not explicitly observe in the Declaration was that the outside world was expected to collaborate actively in the winning of American independence.

Over six months before, on 19 November 1775, the Continental Congress had established a Committee of Secret Correspondence "for the sole purpose of corresponding with our friends in Great Britain, Ireland, and other parts of the world." The results of this correspondence should have been support of the Revolution from such foreign parts as France and Russia. Confidence in their powers of persuasion gave weak and untried American colonists strength to challenge the might of the British empire. Their weapons were not merely the arms hidden in Concord or seized at Fort Ticonderoga, but the enlightened elite of England and France influenced by the preachings of *philosophes* who ought to rally to the defense of the natural rights of the American part of mankind, if not of the national rights of overseas

Englishmen improperly deprived of their liberties. If this appeal should fail, the Congress would remind Europeans of the balance of power and of the advantages which might accrue to France or Spain or Russia from Britain's loss of the American colonies.

Convinced of the successful outcome of these appeals, Congress issued a plan for a model treaty on 17 September 1776. It sketched the ideal relationship between the Old and New Worlds and was to serve as a guide to American diplomatists abroad.

The essays presented in this volume examine the role which the Old World was expected to play in United States foreign affairs, measure expectations against results, and observe the effect of the Revolutionary diplomatic experience upon the growth of American isolationism. The topics dwell on the relationship during the war with the mother country, Great Britain, with the ally France, and with the other European powers more cautiously connected with the Revolution through the anti-British League of Armed Neutrals.

Of all the connections, the relationship with Britain was the most complicated. Britain's fury with American resistance was matched by its bewilderment over its inability to comprehend the sources of America's discontent. That the colonies had developed into a nation with its separate experience was beyond the understanding of the British government. Carl B. Cone's essay reassesses the role of George III, who spoke for the British constitutional system rather than for tyranny; his weaknesses reflected those of his countrymen. Want of understanding would have doomed even the best intentioned missions of reconciliation, as Allen S. Brown observes in his study of the North Ministry's attempts to bring the colonies back to the Empire during the war.

Relations with France lacked the emotional content that dominated the Anglo-American connection. France had been the enemy of American colonies as well as of England until 1763, and if it was now to be a friend, that friendship was an act of conscious statecraft, not unmixed with guile, rather than an outpouring of natural sentiment. The Model Treaty, reassessed by James H. Hutson, was clearly aimed at France. Money, manpower, and national resources were all desired from France, but the alliance and cobelligerency that would follow was not to be accompanied by any American commitment to France. It should be enough that victory over England would redound to France's economic and political advantage in future contests. The United States should not have to bind itself to another European nation, with all the dangers that connection might bring, to win military involvement of the French monarchy. William C. Stinchcombe presents the difference between the ideal of the Model Treaty and the reality of the Franco-American alliance of 1778 as it was experienced by the Continental Congress. The alliance was an entangling alliance, and yet the decision emerges as the wisdom of necessity. To John Adams, however, the Model Treaty continued to hold aloft principles that differentiated the New World from the Old.

David M. Griffiths and Gregg L. Lint deal with countries and problems that were peripheral to the mainstream of the Revolution, but which had beneficial effects on the course of peacemaking. Catherine of Russia misunderstood the nature of the Revolution, and while her support was minimal, it was genuine. It was based on a temporary estrangement from Russia's natural ally, Great Britain. The claims of the Enlightenment were called upon to win a modified blessing to a country's struggle that was fundamentally subversive to the Russian regime. Only after the French Revolution broke out did Catherine turn retrospectively to a negative judgment of the American Revolution as the progenitor of Jacobinism. A Russia hostile to the United States might have prevented the formation of a league to curb British power over the seas. While the League of Armed Neutrals had little effect on the conduct of the British war, the pervasive hostility to Britain that it represented helped create a climate for peace in 1783. Even if Americans misperceived the realities of the law of nations in the eighteenth century, they established bases for future policy. Besides, they would not have to pay the price of misperception until the Anglo-French wars of the 1790s. In the meantime, Britain was isolated in Europe. Out of the climate produced by the Model Treaty and by the professions of the Armed Neutrals came the Treaty of Paris, establishing an independent United States of America. Diplomacy played an important part in securing it, as these essays reveal.

In an epilogue on the significance of the Franco-American alliance, Lawrence S. Kaplan looks at the experience of Revolutionary diplomacy as a source of American isolationism. Relations with Europe, and with France in particular, helped to win independence, but they also convinced Americans of the next generation that entanglement with Europe produced by the alliance of 1778 was to be avoided in the future. When that alliance terminated in 1800, the United States would not enter into another entangling alliance with European nations until the North Atlantic Treaty of 1949.

It is fitting to acknowledge at this time the contributions which a number of scholars in the field offered at the conference on each of the papers. Alison Gilbert Olson of the University of Maryland and Jack M. Sosin of the University of Nebraska at Lincoln commented on the Anglo-American relationship. Lawrence S. Kaplan of Kent State University and Marvin R. Zahniser of Ohio State University served as commentators on Franco-American relations. Paul A. Varg of Michigan State University and Albert H. Bowman of the University of Tennessee at Chattanooga spoke on the "Other Parts of the World." Many of their views have been incorporated into the published versions of the authors' essays.

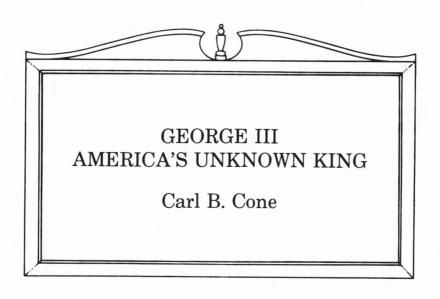

# GEORGE III
# AMERICA'S UNKNOWN KING

## Carl B. Cone

During the long reign of George III, the disparity between the theory and practice of the British Constitution perceptibly widened. For many reasons the immediate headship of the executive was passing from the sovereign to the prime minister. Because this change came experientially and gradually, the period was one of "mixed character." With "the past and the future, capable of neat definition," impinging upon this period, the kingship partook to some extent of both the royal government of earlier times and the parliamentary government of a later time.[1]

With mixed government it was difficult to know who actually determined the policies of what people called (and still do) His (or Her) Majesty's government. Even in simpler situations we cannot always know precisely who shapes and makes decisions. When the king did not always in fact have quite as much authority as his office was supposed constitutionally to possess, and when, like George III, he sometimes "yielded easy assent to ministers" who in crises could "compel" his "favour," the problem of defining the king's role becomes even more difficult.

Against this background is located George III's part in

the making of policies and laws affecting Americans during the decade before the great separation.

Following the Stamp Act of 1765, amidst increasing strain between Britain and her American colonies and deepening bitterness all around, Americans consistently spoke respectfully of and to their king in public declarations. The Stamp Act Congress in its Address to the king spoke of his "sacred person and government." In 1768 the Massachusetts General Court addressed George III as "our common head and father." In August 1774, the Virginia Convention called themselves "dutiful and loyal subjects." In October the Continental Congress asserted their "allegiance" to their king. Later they prayed humbly and dutifully to him for redress of their grievances and soon after fighting began, the Congress, speaking of "the tyranny of irritated ministers," blamed them, not the king, for the troubles that beset the empire. In the autumn of 1775, when replying to the Royal Proclamation declaring the colonies in a state of rebellion, Congress repudiated allegiance to Parliament while still acknowledging their duty to their king.

Whether these deferential forms of address expressed American convictions or were merely observances of proprieties, whether Americans were distinguishing between ministers and king as a divisive tactic, the words used in *official* discourse say literally that up to the fateful year of 1776 Americans did not express animosity toward George III as a king or a person.

In the Declaration of Independence, Jefferson scorned euphemisms though he left room for interpretations. When he spoke of a persistent "design" in Britain to form "an absolute Tyranny" over the American States, and when he saw this sinister design as "the history of the present King of Great Britain," he made George III a party to these schemes or, in a charitable view, a victim of crafty ministers who intended to deprive Americans of their God-given rights as men.

2

In either character, as a dupe or a monster, the king served a purpose. Jefferson led the public then and since to see George III as an active promoter and the intended beneficiary of the conspiracy against American freedom. This character of the king seems fixed in the American mind, and probably will be so for a long time to come. Scholarly reconsiderations never quite engage the public mind. Annually a certain Irish-American parish priest unburdens himself in his St. Patrick's day tirade against the British and their monster king who concentrated in himself the evil Britain represented to Irish and American minds. Why should an Irishman pick on George III in preference to any sovereign from Elizabeth I to Victoria? Probably because, already conditioned to think ill of any British monarch, Irish-Americans have the exquisite pleasure of piling upon their Irish heritage the sense of grievance felt in their other country against that evil man who wronged both peoples.

What the bicentennial observances will do in the long run to the reputation of George III can only be guessed at. In 1976, patriotic impulses clothed in the uniforms of soldiers of the Continental army or the buckskins of Indian fighters stimulated emotional revivals that might strengthen the tradition of George III as the first great national enemy. At times, other national enemies have been useful, Kaiser Bill or Emperor Hirohito. But we have, it appears, forgiven Hirohito, and most emphatically when he rode in an open carriage through the streets of Colonial Williamsburg. Memory of the Kaiser no longer moves us except to scorn and laughter, or pity. But George III, with characteristic obstinacy, hangs in there, and as a people we almost admire him for that. While giving us himself to detest, he remains as a symbol of one view of our revolutionary beginning as a nation—a young virtuous people struggling against an evil system, breaking from it, and then setting out as a new nation along the paths of righteousness on their way west to fulfill the national destiny.

3

Jefferson did his job to perfection. He did not stand outside events, depicting them objectively or dispassionately as a scholar recounting historical truth. He was a public man presenting a case, defending an action, justifying a cause, and George III was conveniently useful as a personification of everything British that Americans in 1776 abhorred. Jefferson was more effective attacking a man or a king rather than a body of men, a parliament or the British cabinet. Everyone spoke according to form and in partially literal constitutional truth of His Majesty's government or His Majesty's servants, so why not place the onus upon His Majesty? Did not the Cabinet only offer advice to the king, meaning, seemingly, that he made the decisions? Technically Jefferson was correct, for by 1776 the authority of Parliament having already been repudiated, the Crown, or the King, was the sole remaining constitutional tie with Britain that Americans admitted. The final act to complete the separation from the mother country was denial of allegiance to the Crown. The Declaration of Independence did just that and gave a long list of reasons.

But there remains the question of the king's responsibility for bringing about such a state of affairs and it raises the problem of the nature of the kingship at this time in its history. The policies and the specific laws Americans objected to were those of the king's government and of the imperial Parliament, which in the fullest legal sense consisted of King, Lords, and Commons. Jefferson knew much about government and his reference in the Declaration to a grand design could have been meant broadly and inclusively rather than personally. But he worded the document so skillfully that a reader could understand him to be attacking the king, and that is the way Americans have preferred to read the Declaration for the past two hundred years.

George III, as a reigning sovereign not yet reduced to political impotence, had broad responsibility for the

4

policies and actions of his government. In effect the king agreed in 1779 when he confessed at a special cabinet meeting that the greatest mistake he had made since he came to the throne was to consent to the repeal of the Stamp Act, for from repeal came all subsequent troubles with America.[2] That is, the king was saying he had the power to prevent his government either from doing wrong or from making mistakes, and in 1766 he did neither when against his instinctive judgment he acquiesced in the cabinet's decision to seek repeal of the Stamp Act. If the king did not prevent passage of bills by Lords and Commons, these bills only became statutes when the king signed them. The royal veto was not yet constitutionally dead, nor did the king think it was obsolete.[3] If he disliked strongly enough any of the American legislation, at the risk of creating a domestic crisis he might constitutionally have vetoed it. In discussing with Lord North his answer to the City of London Address against the Quebec Act in 1774, the king said he desired to avoid language that might be taken to mean he would never use the veto against a measure objectionable to him.[4] But he approved of the Quebec Act, thus exhibiting a greater tolerance for Roman Catholics than some of his New England subjects, such as, for example, the Reverend Ezra Stiles who thought the Act would please the Papists and set off a "Jubilee in Hell."[5]

It is necessary to define the king's role in events leading up to the American Revolution to appreciate how much or how little George III conformed to the simplistic American tradition. The enactment of a statute or the enunciation of a governmental policy then, as now, was the culmination of a complex and sometimes long sequence beginning with the recognition of a public need or problem and involving the labor and time of many people along the way. At various stages of the sequence George III might, constitutionally, intrude by suggesting, by approving or disapproving, or even by influencing or directing men's thoughts and actions.[6]

The king rarely attended cabinet meetings. The earliest date on which he met with the cabinet was 21 June 1779. He saw cabinet members individually and routinely in the closet, where business relating to individual departments might be discussed before a minister laid it before the cabinet. The king also corresponded with his ministers on departmental business or cabinet discussions. The practice of reporting to the king by regular cabinet minutes was not routine until after 1778.[7]

Recent studies of the cabinet in this period disagree in their conclusions about the king's relationship to it. Ian Christie presents a king less dominating than Richard Pares's and more active *vis à vis* the cabinet than Sir Lewis Namier's.[8] Christie rejects the label "personal rule" as descriptive of George III's reign in the period of the American Revolution. He finds the king engaged in "constant dialogue over policy" with the cabinet or individual ministers, but this means more that the king liked to know what was going on than that he was telling the cabinet what to do. Similarly, when a minister in North's departmentalized government took the initiative in ascertaining the royal pleasure before referring departmental business to the whole cabinet for collective decision, he was keeping the king informed. In moments of crisis, as in 1774, "the cabinet as a whole was in constant control of developments." Broadly speaking, the cabinet had "a considerable momentum of its own. The king did not shape ministries to conform to his views of policy; the king might be expected to follow the wishes or advice of ministers; they sometimes accepted royal suggestions; but the cabinet was the "real effective center of decision." To sum up, the king was involved with policy-making in no uniform or consistent way but variously, as circumstances differed, and rarely decisively.[9]

Reference to specific matters relating to America will illustrate and clarify this summary. We know much about the Stamp Act. Articles by Edmund S. Morgan and

Charles R. Ritcheson some twenty years ago traced the evolution of the Act from inception of the idea to enactment as law. Except for an indirect reference to the king in a letter written by Franklin in 1778 and quoted in part by Morgan, neither scholar mentions the king.[10] Morgan's quotation reveals that in retrospect Franklin doubted whether the king had any part in the framing or enactment of the law. Christie cites a letter to Bute in March 1763 as evidence that the king was "fully in touch" with American revenue conversations at that time and he also refers to Horace Walpole's later version of an account, told him in 1780 by a kinsman of Grenville, of the king's strong endorsement of the stamp tax.[11] The latest study by P. D. G. Thomas assigns to the king no more of a role than the earlier ones did. This information suggests something that will apply to the Intolerable Acts of 1774. The king did not initiate the idea of a stamp tax, nor was he directly involved in transforming the idea into a statute, but he knew of the proceedings and presumably approved. Something we do not know of may have passed on the subject in the closet and it is a fair presumption that if the king's approbation was known, it may indirectly have influenced voting in the Lords and Commons. This conjecture becomes stronger when we consider that during the interval between the sessions of 1764 and 1765 Americans raised questions about Britain's right to tax, and parliamentary consideration of the Stamp Act was transformed into an assertion of parliamentary supremacy.[12] If so, the king's approval was assured, for he was more concerned with supremacy than with revenues. At any rate, the king's servants framed the bill, the imperial Parliament passed it and the king signed it, and so the king was ultimately responsible for the Stamp Act in the general sense described earlier.

On the subject of Stamp Act repeal the king finally expressed himself in a manner that confused members of Parliament but he did not take an active part in securing repeal. The Rockingham cabinet made the decision to

seek repeal and to accompany it with an act declaratory
of Britain's right, and the king acquiesced, though he
personally preferred to repeal or enforcement an amend-
ment of the Act in some form that might make it less
distasteful to Americans while preserving Britain's
legislative supremacy.[13] When the question became
polarized, the king preferred repeal to enforcement. The
king "as usual" left formulation of policy to the ministry,
saying only that he wanted government to be "firm,"
refusing either to betray his ministers or to try to
influence members, except Lord Northington, in their
parliamentary opinions when Rockingham supporters
(unwhiggishly?) were ready to welcome royal influence in
support of repeal.[14] Eight years later Burke recalled that
"a partial repeal, or as the *bon-ton* of the court then was, a
*modification*" was a "resource of weak, undeciding
minds." After careful study of alternatives the administration took its plan of repeal to Parliament which
approved "by an independent, noble, spirited, and
unexpected majority."[15]

I have no evidence that the king resented Burke's term
"weak, undeciding minds," but if he noticed it and
thought it applied to him, he should have objected, for he
was proud of his firmness of views and resolution
throughout the years of the American controversy. Yet in
this instance Burke was right, for the king was indecisive
in 1766, and that was the reason why politicians were
puzzled as to what were his views. And the king admitted
this in 1779. In 1766 the king's dilemma was everyone's
dilemma and it proved impossible for men to agree on
some magic formula that would satisfy everyone on both
sides of the Atlantic. Statesmen of the era could not find
ground on which British rights and American rights, or
both sides' conceptions of their rights, could flourish or
even exist simultaneously and in harmony one with the
other. In the larger view the imperial quarrel was a great
classic tragedy. George III was unfortunate enough to be
on the throne when a problem insoluble in any terms

politically acceptable to that generation confronted his subjects in the Old and the New Worlds.

A nineteenth-century biographer of the king, John Heneage Jesse, says that George III could have prevented repeal if he had worked against it, and Burke's description of the majority which carried repeal as "unexpected" suggests the same idea.[16] Both opponents and proponents of repeal said the king favored their positions even though the king refused to influence parliamentary opinions. We know that men speculated about the king's view and Rockingham was anxious for the king's ultimate endorsement of repeal to be known, for conflicting tales were bandied about concerning the king's remarks on the subject to Rockingham and Lord Strange. The king's refusal to coerce placeholders into supporting repeal—because for the moment Rockingham's was the king's government—was also well known. And so the uncertainty in men's minds was great until finally repeal carried.

The government found a compromise acceptable to a majority in Parliament, though it could not satisfy Americans once the first enthusiasm over repeal wore off. The Declaratory Act which accompanied repeal said plainly that Britain had the right to tax the Americans even though the word "tax" does not appear in the Act, entitled "an act for the better securing the dependency of his majesty's dominions in America upon the crown and Parliament of Great Britain." The act declared that Parliament "had, hath, and of right ought to have full power" to legislate for the colonies "in all cases whatsoever," and "in all cases" clearly included tax laws. Pitt, of course, objected because he would not admit the power to tax America, holding as he did the feudal notion of an extraordinary aid as a free gift requiring direct consent. But Pitt stood almost alone on his medieval ground.

Pleased to think tranquillity restored, the king approved the assertion of Britain's constitutional authority over America. He blamed the tactless Grenville for the late unpleasantness. Having restrained their trade, he said, Grenville deprived Americans of the means of "acquiring wealth" and then he taxed them.[17] The king said this in 1767, but as early as December 1765 when American protests against the Stamp Tax were reaching England, he spoke sarcastically to the Duke of Grafton of Grenville's *"wise regulations"* (italics his) for executing the Stamp Act.[19] The king's private letters to Grafton make one wonder whether someone strained the truth in Walpole's version of Grenville's story of the king's approval of the Stamp Tax. Or possibly when it was all over, the king's accumulated dislike of "Greenville" (as he often wrote the name) controlled his memory.

The Declaratory Act, that "masterpiece" of the Rock-inghams as Pares somewhere described it, did not represent only their opinions. It stated British constitutional orthodoxy as it was grounded on the idea of parliamentary sovereignty, and it was that orthodoxy which the king upheld when he saw his constitutional duty during the controversy with America as the maintenance of the rights of Parliament.[19] This doctrine enjoyed the determined support of nearly all members of Parliament; of eminent legal authorities such as Black-stone and Lord Mansfield; of pamphleteers as weighty as Samuel Johnson and John Wesley; of the public generally in the years before the war; and of the king. If it removed doubts about authoritative and official opinion in Britain, the act nevertheless became a mischievous, even pernicious measure. It frustrated efforts to find a compromise with American views until all hope of reconciliation was dead because it made clear that any modification would appear at once as a surrender to American intransigence. Britain chose a forward legal position from which an attack might be repelled, but failing that, withdrawal would be tantamount to defeat. Britain occupied the position until war began and then the Americans abandoned their attacks upon Britain's legal defenses, outflanked them, and engaged the enemy on philosophical ground, shouting their battle cry of the rights of men.

But prior to that climax the Bostonians held a Tea Party. When on 29 January 1774 the cabinet decided formally on a policy of firmness toward America, they knew the king would approve.[20] Promptly, as he always was prompt to respond, he approved the "'unanimous advice'" of his cabinet favoring measures "'for securing the dependence of the colonies upon this kingdom.'"[21]

Their general understanding of the king's position may have influenced members of Parliament when they voted on the bills that together became known as the Intolerable Acts, but the precise extent of that influence cannot be measured. As consideration of the bills proceeded, the king in the closet and in letters forcefully expressed his desire to see Britain's supremacy maintained. He was closer to the positions of Suffolk, Gower, and Sandwich, the least flexible men in the cabinet, than he was to the moderate colonial secretary, Dartmouth, or to North, who needed his reassurances.

Unlike the Stamp Act and the Quebec Act, which were preceded by careful and protracted study, the Intolerable Acts were drafted hastily and passed quickly through Parliament during the next three months. Though he played no direct part, the king blessed the work and watched proceedings closely. North's comfortable majorities carried the bills and after the king signed them, he confidently expected the "speedy submission" of the colonies when they felt the effects of the new legislation.[22]

Because the king was so clearly on top of events the impression comes easily that he was the ringmaster cracking the whip. Governor Hutchinson, in London at the time, knew from talking with him that the king had a detailed knowledge of American affairs. (The king had a mind for details and minutiae on a variety of subjects.) Hutchinson thought the king was his own minister.[23] Similarly, but thinking beyond the American legislation,

11

Pares, twenty years ago, could ask seriously whether George III was Prime Minister at this time.[24]

Can we be more precise than to say that George III was an "active" king in the period leading up to the American Revolution?[25] Some activity is merely busywork, and other activity produces results. Some of the evidence adduced as proof of the king's activity only details his efforts to keep informed or ministers' efforts to keep him informed. It was well understood that the king insisted on knowing what was going on in Parliament, the cabinet, and the administration. He hungered for this kind of knowledge, often as an end in itself. In 1800-01, Pitt the Younger forgot this, either unintentionally or deliberately. The documents relating to union with Ireland, Catholic Emancipation, and Pitt's resignation in 1801 persuade me that the king was terribly hurt because Pitt kept things from him and he reacted strongly when belatedly he learned of them, not only because he opposed Emancipation but because he had not been treated as a king had a constitutional right to be treated.

Of other relations with the cabinet in the 1760s and 1770s, Christie concludes that the king nearly always submitted to the cabinet's advice, even when it was contrary to his own judgment; when ministers' opinions were divided, the king might tip the balance.[26] But we must remember that on American questions up to the outbreak of war, unanimity prevailed in the cabinet, and between it and the king, and near unanimity in Parliament and the country on the basic questions of parliamentary constitutional supremacy. With only two statutes was the king directly and dominantly involved in this period, the Regency Act of 1765 and the Royal Marriages Act of 1772, and they were of quite a separate order. Normally the king made little positive contribution to the process of decision making; his influence, if and when it existed, was indirect and was simply in the air because his basic position was well known, as for example his approval (and the general approval) of the

Declaratory Act of 1766 was a constant conditioning influence enveloping all consideration of the American question while the act was in force.

The harmony between king, cabinet and the parliamentary majority after 1770 and during the first five years of the American war gave a misleading appearance to policy and decision making. The fundamental statement of constitutional policy toward America was the Declaratory Act of 1766, and as long as Britain adhered to it, which was until 1778, the king did not have to direct actively even had he been so inclined. He could and did encourage his ministers and approve their actions, and he could approve readily because those actions were such as he might have advised himself to take. The Intolerable Acts pleased him because they were compatible with his view and the nation's view of the imperial constitution and with his belief that firmness would bring the colonies to submit at the same time that he was doing his constitutional duty under God to preserve the lawful authority of Parliament and the integrity of the British Empire. He gave a lead to the nation as simultaneously he was following the nation's lead, for with the exception of a small minority at large and a measurable minority in Parliament, George III was king of a united nation with a united government.

The Americans had often addressed their king as a father, and the British thought of the colonies as children. In 1767, replying to an address from the Massachusetts Assembly thanking him for carrying repeal of the Stamp Act when he headed the government, the Marquis of Rockingham wrote to Massachusetts, "'I shall always consider, that this country, as the parent, ought to be tender and just, and that the colonies, as the children, ought to be dutiful.'"27

The form was appropriate, such as the king might have used. But his view of fatherhood differed slightly from the childless Rockingham's. The king and Queen Charlotte had 15 children. George III thought of the colonies as

13

dependencies, immature, requiring parental guidance, and owing submission to their father and to their mother country. As later with his own disorderly sons, he would be a father to his American subjects and as a good father should do, teach them obedience. He would be stern, even severely so, in their own best interest, and that was because he loved them. But George was not a successful father. His relations with his sons were unpleasant and unhappy, as his relations with his American children turned out to be. Literally and symbolically, George III failed as a father. The qualities that made him an unsuccessful father to his own children made him an unsuccessful father to his American children. But it should be said that his children at home and across the Atlantic had a capacity for being hard to deal with—a bit spoiled, resentful of restraints yet remarkably free of them, precocious in some respects and puerile in others, they were altogether too much for an exasperated and frustrated father to understand. Fathers and children, alas, often misunderstand one another.

## NOTES

1. Sir Lewis Namier, *Crossroads of Power* (New York: Macmillan, 1962), pp. 214-15, 217, 226, and for the quotations in the next paragraph.

2. Historical Manuscripts Commission Reports, *Various Collections*, VI (1909), H. V. Knox MSS., 260.

3. Sir John Fortescue, ed., *The Correspondence of King George the Third from 1760 to December, 1783* (London: Macmillan, 1928), III, #1481, the King to Lord North, 19 June 1774.

4. Ibid.

5. *Proceedings of the Massachusetts Historical Society* (May and June 1903), p. 282, Stiles to Dr. Richard Price, 10 April 1775.

6. In 1765 he suggested a change after reading an early draft of the American Mutiny Act. Grenville disregarded the king's advice and encountered trouble in the Commons on the point the king warned him against. P.D.G. Thomas, *British Politics and the Stamp Act Crisis* (Oxford: Clarendon Press, 1975), pp. 102-08.

7. Ian R. Christie, *Myth and Reality in Late Eighteenth-Century England and Other Papers* (Berkeley: Univ. of California Press, 1970), pp. 81-83.

8. Pares, *George III and the Politicians* (London: Oxford Univ. Press Paperback, 1967), esp. Chap. V; Namier, *Crossroads*, esp. Chaps. 7, 9, and 20; Christie, *Myth and Reality*, esp. Chap. II.

9. Pares, *George III and the Politicians*, pp. 12, 13, 65, 71, 72, 84, 90-91, 93-94, 98. Also Thomas, *British Politics*, pp. 21-26.

10. Morgan, "The Postponement of the Stamp Act," *William and Mary Quarterly*, Ser. 3, 7 (1950), 353-92, and the quotation from Franklin, 391; Ritcheson, "The Preparation of the Stamp Act," *William and Mary Quarterly*, Ser. 3, 10 (1953), 543-59.

11. *Myth and Reality*, pp. 97-98; Romney Sedwick, ed., *Letters from George III to Lord Bute, 1756-1766* (London: Macmillan, 1939), pp. 201-02; Horace Walpole's *Last Journals*, ed. A. F. Steuart (London: J. Lane, 1910), II, 337-38, n. 1.

12. Jack M. Sosin, *Whitehall and the Wilderness* (Lincoln: Univ. of Nebraska Press, 1961), pp. 86-88 and Thomas, *British Politics*, pp. 51 ff., 61, 76, 79.

13. British Museum, Add. MS. 35430, ff. 31-32, Rockingham to Charles Yorke, 17 [19] Jan. 1766; Fortescue, ed., *Corr.*, I (1927), #247, #248. For a detailed discussion of the intricacies and confusion of the king's position, see Thomas, *British Politics*, pp. 164-247, passim.

14. Thomas, *British Politics*, pp. 164-65, 186, 228, 235, 241-43, 246.

15. "Speech on American Taxation," *Works* (Boston: Little, Brown and Company, 1884), II, 48-49.

16. *Memoirs of the Court of England: The Life and Reign of King George the Third* (Boston: Chester F. Rice Company, n.d.), II, 23, 26-27.

17. West Suffolk Record Office, Grafton Papers 423/490, the King to Grafton, 24 Feb. 1767.

18. *Ibid.*, 423/482, same to same, 17 Dec. 1765. Franklin B. Wickwire, *British Subministers and Colonial America 1763-1783* (Princeton: Princeton Univ. Press, 1966) pp. 106-09, 190-93, criticizes Grenville for ineptness in making, or failing to make, arrangements for executing the Stamp Act.

19. Bernard Donoughue, *British Politics and the American Revolution: The Paths to War 1773-1775* (London: Macmillan, 1964), pp. 41-42.

20. *Ibid.*, p. 34.

21. Lord Dartmouth to Governor William Tryon, 5 Feb. 1774, quoted in R. D. Bargar, *Lord Dartmouth and the American Revolution* (Columbia: Univ. of S. Carolina Press, 1965), p. 106.

22. Fortescue, ed., *Corr.*, III #1486, the King to Lord North, 1 July 1774.

23. Donoughue, *British Politics*, p. 163.

24. *George III*, pp. 174-75.

25. Donoughue, *British Politics*, p. 284.

26. *Myth and Reality*, pp. 209-10.

27. Quoted in Thomas, *British Politics*, p. 371.

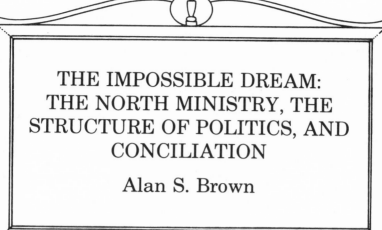

# THE IMPOSSIBLE DREAM: THE NORTH MINISTRY, THE STRUCTURE OF POLITICS, AND CONCILIATION

## Alan S. Brown

Although Anglo-American relations were to get worse, by 1769 they were already strained enough to cause at least one Englishman to cry plaintively: "Can no body propose a Plan of Conciliation?" Benjamin Franklin, to whom this particular plea was addressed, had a ready answer: "*Repeal* the Laws, *Renounce* the Right, *Recall* the Troops, *Refund* the Money, and *Return to the old Method of Requisition.*" This was not only the shortest and most alliterative conciliatory plan on record, it also had much to recommend it. But while Franklin's friend could accept most of the terms, one point nettled, and he asked: "But why would you insist on our Renouncing the Right?" Franklin's answer, both wise and witty, was unacceptable then and in subsequent years. He said, "I do not insist upon that, . . . if continuing the Claim pleases you, continue it as long as you please provided you never attempt to execute it. We shall consider it in the same light with the Claim of the Spanish Monarch to the Title of King of Jerusalem."[1]

Franklin's proposal may have been one of the wisest, but it was clearly not the last. In the years following 1769 the British government, the Continental Congress, and numerous individuals in Parliament and out, were to offer a variety of conciliatory plans. But for the British

17

only three of these plans were official. These were Lord North's Conciliatory Resolution of 1775, the Howe Commission of 1776, and the Carlisle Commission of 1778. For a variety of reasons, none of the British offers was ever seriously considered by the Americans, but these responses, amply discussed elsewhere, are not a primary concern of this paper.[2] It is proposed, however, that an analysis of these three conciliatory moves by the British during the American Revolution, and of the milieu in which they were produced, may yield a few more grains of insight on why England acted as she did, and provide a better appreciation of the limits within which the ministers who faced the crisis had to work as they sought to prevent dismemberment of the first British Empire.

The idea is often advanced that on several occasions prior to the Declaration of Independence, and especially after the repeal of the Townshend duties, a relatively lasting Anglo-American accord could have been reached if only the British government had made a constitutional gesture that recognized the growth, aspirations, and maturity of the colonies.[3] Such a move, it is argued, would have formalized the sort of federal relationship that Franklin and a few others had privately envisaged, and which, unrecognized by the British, had been evolving in the empire over many years. But no ministers, not even Chatham or Burke had they headed the government, could have made that kind of constitutional rearrangement.[4] In fact it would have been impossible, Sir Lewis Namier reminded us, because "Great Britain had not yet reached the stage at which it would have been possible to remodel the Empire as a federation of self-governing States under a Crown detached from the actual government of any of its component parts." Since the crown was still an active force in politics, "any exercise of its attributes apart from the British Parliament would have seemed a dangerous and unconstitutional reversion to 'prerogative'." Thus, Namier continued, "this junction between King and Parliament was by itself bound to carry the supremacy of the British Parliament into the Colonies; and the very fact that George III so thoroughly and loyally stood by the constitutional principles of the time rendered a conflict inevitable...."[5]

In brief, it was the responsibility of George III and the North ministry to govern the British Empire on the basis of a constitution that gave primacy to the concept of parliamentary supremacy. Further, the ministry, in the fashion of eighteenth-century ministries, would seek a specific solution for each problem as it developed.[6] Thus, after the repeal of the Townshend duties and prior to the Tea Act, it is unrealistic to expect that the North ministry would have proposed measures for America that were directed to root causes of discontent, or which aimed at sweeping reform of existing relationships. The government would uphold parliamentary supremacy if it was challenged, but at the same time it hoped no major disturbance would arise to disrupt the empire.

But if the government hoped for no troubles in America, it had no intention of abdicating authority there either. Thus, when the North ministry faced the crisis brought on by the tangled finances of the East India Company, it did not hesitate to employ a solution to the problem that also involved the American colonies. But the ministry's hopes that Americans would accept the Tea Act because tea was now cheaper were blasted when news of the Boston Tea Party reached London early in 1774.

Confronted by this challenge, for it was so regarded, what would the ministry do—what could it do? It could, and did, rule out conciliatory moves or concessions of any sort. Without doubt this would have been its course even if George III had not reminded Lord North "that the fatal compliance in 1766" had encouraged the Americans to annually move further from "the obedience which a Colony owes to its Mother Country."[7] The government decided that steps should "be taken to secure the Dependence of the Colonies on the Mother Country,"[8] and proceeded energetically with a series of measures known as the Coercive Acts. These were a logical and consistent stance for Britain to take—the authority of Parliament had been defied, and all the ministers were agreed on that point. Given the nature of the constitutional and political beliefs that British ministers operated from there was no other course that made sense. A colony had gotten out of its proper imperial relationship and the government had a duty to correct this.[9]

From the standpoint of conciliatory prospects the ministry's response to the Tea Party is instructive, for that crisis shows much as to British expectations, understanding of the Americans, and the limitations on British actions. First of all, the government felt it *had* to respond. Lord Dartmouth, more inclined to conciliation than the other ministers, was nonetheless emphatic here: "The question then is whether these laws are to be submitted to? If the people of America say no, they say in effect they will no longer be part of the British Empire. . . ." To Dartmouth there was no middle ground, if "neither Parliament nor America will recede, the most dreadful consequences will ensue." But Dartmouth, hoping to conciliate, sought to convince Americans that all that Britain really asked was submission to Parliament's authority, to admit parliamentary right, which included the power to tax, and that having made this submission they could take it on faith that the power would not be used, and "peace and harmony be restored to this. . . most unhappily divided and distracted empire." Dartmouth's attitude here reflected what would be a constant in future offers to negotiate with the Americans: the British government insisted on submission—after that, discussion of other points could follow. Joseph Reed, with whom Dartmouth was exploring conciliatory approaches, was shocked: "Such is Lord Dartmouth's confession of faith,—bad enough God knows! But if he thinks thus, what may we expect from Hillsborough and the rest!"[10]

Another aspect of the ministry's, and Dartmouth's, reaction here is worth noting. The information they received from America, and the way they interpreted it, tended to prevent them from gauging the depth of American feelings and the real strength of opposition to British policy. Most of the government's information came from officials in America, which is not unusual, but there is no indication that the ministers ever intended to evaluate data on the basis of its source. The result was that the ministry habitually underestimated American union while emphasizing the factious nature of colonial resistance. All through the course of events, from pre-Lexington days to the end of the war, no British minister showed sufficient realization of the fact that American leaders were more than a handful of radicals, and that American resistance was more than a civil disturbance.[11] Further, this attitude bears directly on the British failure to make official conciliatory proposals in 1774. If the source of trouble was simply a handful of rabble, would it not be easier and more effective to bring them back to order by coercion rather than by conciliatory gestures?

The Coercive Acts helped to unite the Americans and were the major factor in the movement that led to the Continental Congress in September 1774. While this body was deliberating, and before England learned of its actions, George III noted approval of the course taken by the British government. There was no reason, he wrote, for England to

> give way to the opinions of North America; the dye is now cast, the Colonies must either submit or triumph; I do not wish to come to severer measures but we must not retreat; by coolness and an unremitted pursuit of the measures that have been adopted I trust they will come to submit; I have no objections afterwards to their seeing that there is no inclination for the present to lay fresh taxes on them, but I am clear there must always be one tax to keep up the right, and as such I approve of the Tea Duty.[12]

This well-known statement is quoted at length to provide emphasis to several points that must be remembered in evaluating the British government's responses to American developments. George III was the most important figure in the government, and ministers rarely went against his wishes. And even if this had not been the case, his opinion on the American question did not differ from his ministry's. More than anything else, the king believed it his duty to uphold the constitution, and the Americans had defied that constitution. His insistence, and hope, that they would submit was not an isolated reaction: it was shared by the entire ministry and most of Parliament, in short, by the entire British political nation.[13] Later, when conciliatory proposals were made, they all included the point of submission, and the only real arguments any of the ministers ever had on this was concerning the timing. Was submission to be obtained prior to discussions, or could it be made during the course of them?

The ministry was not idle as it awaited news from the colonies, and from Massachusetts in particular. Warships and marines were dispatched to Boston, prohibitions were enacted on the export of arms and munitions to America, and Parliament was dissolved and new elections scheduled.[14] The use of armed force was openly discussed, and if few were as firmly determined as the king, with his statement that "blows must decide whether [the New England colonies] are to be subject to this Country or independent . . .," no voice of any consequence was raised either in support of the Americans or against the possibility of force.[15] In addition, General Gage's supposed lack of vigor in Massachusetts came under increased criticism, and the possibility of replacing him with a more active commander was explored.[16]

Slowly but surely the possibilities of any large scale support for the Americans outside of Parliament were closed off, making it unlikely that the ministry would feel any real pressure to develop conciliatory alternatives to its American policy. In previous American crises the parliamentary opposition had received some support

22

from political forces in London, but increasing radicalism in the city tended to alienate followers of Chatham and Rockingham. Mercantile support of the Americans was also in decline as many merchants began to feel that "customers and debtors on the other side of the Atlantic needed to be whipped before they could be relied on to do business quietly." And beyond this, American trade was becoming relatively less important to many English merchants.[17] Another indicator of the loss of mercantile support for the colonies was the fact that colonial agents, once active and reasonably effective, found themselves without any real influence with the ministers or Parliament in the crisis of 1774. Even Franklin, whose reputation at one time was said to give him "a degree of credit little short of *proofs of holy writ*," had suffered a severe loss of prestige and influence because of his role in the Hutchinson letters affair.[18]

News of the Continental Congress and its Association reached London on 13 December 1774, and served to confirm George III and the ministry in their view that the Americans were in rebellion. In addition, letters from General Gage made it clear that the Coercive Acts had only stiffened American resistance, "and united the whole in one common cause." Matters were so serious, he wrote, that his troops, if used, "will encourage Resistance, and not terrify . . . ."[19] The ministry held three cabinets in January at which it decided to restrain New England's shipping, reinforce General Gage and Admiral Graves, and make the first official British move toward reconciliation with the colonies.[20]

That the British would even consider a conciliatory move was highly significant for it meant that the ministry was beginning to appreciate the point that the Americans ought to be told in a more specific way what Britain wanted, or as Dartmouth expressed it, "what is ultimately expected of them."[21] Coercive measures would not be discarded, but if the Americans were given a definite proposal and agreed to it, they could avoid suffering them. The plan to make a conciliatory gesture, and at the same time to back it with an assertion of force set a pattern for British prosecution of the war. Conciliation and coercion were complementary aspects of a policy with one goal: restoration of parliamentary authority in America.[22]

Lord North's Conciliatory Resolution of February 1775, approved shortly after Parliament had turned down Chatham's elaborate plan, was an offer that Parliament would refrain from exercising its right of taxation if the Americans admitted that right, and at the same time raised money for administration and defense through their own assemblies. Further, duties raised in process of trade regulation would be credited to the colonies involved.[23]

In February 1775 it was a major concession for the head of the ministry even to suggest that Parliament would not exercise its right to tax the Americans providing they raised quotas themselves. But the radical nature of North's offer has been overlooked because in defending his position to his own supporters, who thought the bill indicated weakness, North made statements that suggested he really intended no concessions.[24] And because North's offer did not recognize that the real issue between England and America went far beyond the question of taxation, it is easier to charge him with insincerity. Further, when North either would not or could not unbend to the point of offering his plan to the Continental Congress or make some special effort other than circulating it to the individual American assemblies, it suggests to some that he felt no sense of urgency or any particular reason for using exceptional means to get his plan before the colonists.[25]

Lord North wanted the restoration of Parliament's authority in America, but he now knew that the government's first measures had not worked, hence he and the ministry were ready to use force. But on the chance that a significant number of Americans were not bent on resistance, and because it was possible the colonists failed to understand Britain's position, North thought an offer should be made. In his mind the political side of things took precedence over the military, and he was reluctant to abandon political means even though the use of force was also indicated. His Conciliatory Resolve might succeed in bringing the Americans back to their proper allegiance. And, even if it was not a complete success, it could have the effect of dividing the Americans, which in itself would make Britain's task of restoring obedience easier. In any case he felt his proposition was "precisely the plan which ought to be adopted by Great Britain; even if all America were subdued."[26] In short, Parliamentary supremacy could be retained without the actual exercise of taxation.

The Americans did not take Lord North's Conciliatory Resolve seriously, and with slight exception this has been true for historians ever since. In general their views reflect those expressed by the parliamentary opposition, or Benjamin Franklin, who likened it to the highwayman who sets his own limits on what he takes from his victims.[27] The proposal has been judged inadequate, called a "clumsy attempt to destroy colonial union and pacify dissident Englishmen," and it has also been stated that it was "not even a halfway measure for peace; it was a stupid gesture."[28]

To describe the Conciliatory Resolution as inadequate is no doubt accurate, but other charges against it are too harsh. If the nature of British political ideology and the rigidity of the system is understood, if an attempt is made to understand the pressures North and Dartmouth felt— and if one is willing to give Lord North a minimal benefit of doubt and assume that he was not anxious for war— then it is possible to see the Conciliatory Resolution as a well-intentioned but ineffective measure by a harried minister. In sum, it was not a statesman's gesture, and even if North had been a statesman, the structure of British politics and the degree to which England was

25

committed to parliamentary supremacy would have precluded the sort of proposal Americans could take seriously in 1775.[29]

No other official conciliatory moves were made by the British in 1775, and when news of Lexington and Concord, and Bunker Hill reached England the government knew it was at war with its American colonies. The Americans, once hostilities broke out, did not give reconciliation high priority themselves even though John Dickinson and other moderates were able to get the second Continental Congress to agree to the "Olive Branch Petition," but more reflective of the spirit of that body was its "Declaration of the Causes and Necessity of Taking Up Arms."[30] The British government made its position known by issuing the Royal Proclamation of Rebellion in August, and conciliatory proposals, if they were to be made, would have to await more definite news from America and ministerial rearrangements.[31]

By 26 October, when Parliament convened, it was apparent that Lord North had been active while members vacationed. The king's speech disclosed that the government's plans for America included sending a royal commission to attempt a settlement with the colonies. Lord North had carefully laid the foundation for this move, and he was on much stronger grounds than he had been at the start of the year with his Conciliatory Resolution. The ministry had removed Gage and Graves from command, made arrangements for army and navy increases, was preparing to replace Dartmouth with the aggressive Germain, and in general had been active enough with preparations for bringing the Americans back to allegiance so that no one could accuse it of weakness. If conciliation was tried there would be force enough to remind the colonies of the wisdom of coming back to their duty.[32]

The peace commission now planned and which would eventually be headed by the Howe brothers illustrates in even more striking fashion than North's Conciliatory

Resolution the inability of the British government to break with traditional methods and patterns of thought and behavior. All of the same rigidity of structure, adherence to fixed notions and habitual customs were displayed as Lord North sought to implement his long cherished scheme. Again, as in February 1775, it was obvious that if the British government was to make a conciliatory gesture, such a move would be dictated by what Lord North thought he could manage to get his supporters to accept, not by what he or the ministry thought would be most likely to be taken seriously by the Americans. This is not to suggest that the British offer would be insincere so much as it is to acknowledge that the government was so rigidly intent on parliamentary supremacy, and so careful that none of its moves be interpreted as deviating from it, that one is simply forced to conclude that the North ministry and its supporters were so much the prisoners of their own political structure that it did not occur to them to question whether or not they were engaged in a vain effort.[33]

The discussions and preparations that involved North's legal advisers and assistants reveal how carefully the ministry weighed its offer to the Americans. In the end the only real concession the Howes would be able to make after the commission was arranged was simply a reassertion of North's Resolution of 1775, namely that Parliament would refrain from using its taxing powers if the colonies undertook to raise revenue quotas themselves.[34] Yet Chief Justice Lord Mansfield, Solicitor General Wedderburn, and William Eden all spent hours on this very point, for it came close to the heart of the matter—parliamentary supremacy. Of additional interest here is the fact that, unlike the others, Lord Mansfield actually felt that Britain had to make an offer to the Americans because he doubted her ability to conquer them, but he was still hesitant about compromising Parliament's authority.[35]

But the difficulty over determining whether parliamentary authority was weakened by the concession to refrain from the taxing power was not the only problem the government had in arranging the terms the Howes would carry. The question of how submission to Parliament was to be conveyed proved extremely difficult. Lord North, Germain, Sandwich, Suffolk, and the extreme coercion party in Parliament could all agree that the Americans must put down their arms, dissolve Congress, and restore legal governments. But whereas North felt that such actions in themselves would be an acknowledgement of Parliament's authority, Germain and the cabinet extremists were determined that peace could only come when the colonial assemblies made a full declaration accepting "the supreme authority of the [British] Legislature to make laws binding on the colonies in all cases whatsoever," and that such submission was a prerequisite to negotiations. To get around an impasse Dartmouth and North both talked of resigning from the cabinet, but Germain then said it would be better if *he* resigned. Finally, a compromise was worked out whereby the commissioners would not demand a declaration of submission but instead would await an offer from the colonists, and if no such offer was made, then peace could not be restored.[36] Quite apart from the question of whether there was any likelihood of the Americans making such an offer, this episode again serves to illustrate the rigidity and the fixation on constitutional doctrine of the British government. And, it may be noted, the incident is a splendid example of the government's failure to understand anything of the revolutionary character of the struggle in which it was involved.

There were numerous problems in securing the services of Admiral Richard, Lord Howe, to head the mission despite the fact that he had long sought such a position. Even after arrangements were completed the ministry had difficulty getting him to accept a fellow commissioner, but this was nothing when measured by the difficulties experienced in working out negotiating instructions.[37]

This meant that the government lost a great deal of time between its announcement in October 1775, and May 1776, when Admiral Howe sailed off on his mission. Meanwhile the Americans moved closer to declaring their independence.

The terms the Howes eventually agreed to work under severely limited what could be offered and clearly illustrate the ministry's inability to move beyond traditional patterns of thought and practice. The Americans would be offered peace—but a peace on terms they had already rejected, and based on premises that showed Britain's failure to understand the basic issue of the dispute. The heart of the British proposal was parliamentary supremacy, but the Americans had already discovered popular sovereignty, and were unlikely to take part in discussions that were not binding until reviewed and agreed to by Parliament. In short, the terms the Howe Commission had to offer have been accurately described as "those a victorious and reasonably benevolent mother country might have granted to discouraged and chastised rebels. As such they were totally inadequate to achieve a restoration of peace."[38]

The first two British offers to negotiate with the Americans were based on the premise that Britain had the military force to make conciliation an attractive alternative.[39] This assumption was much less clear at the time of the third British offer, made in 1778, and carried to America by the Carlisle Commission. Even before the full results of British military operations for 1777 were known, Lord North reverted to his hopes of a negotiated peace, and when it appeared that Sir William Howe, at least, was successful North speculated whether Britain should "take advantage of the flourishing state of our affairs to get out of this d—d war, and hold a moderate language?"[40] News of the disaster of Saratoga removed all doubt as to what line to follow. That defeat and the imminent announcement of a Franco-American alliance made another peace attempt imperative.

29

While the ministry absorbed the shock of Burgoyne's defeat Lord North announced that he would introduce measures for reconciliation with America. But when Parliament recessed for the holiday season North learned through secret negotiations conducted in Paris that since Americans enjoyed *de facto* independence they would hardly settle for less. George III, although aware that British strategy must be revised, was reluctant to propose conciliatory measures on grounds that the government's supporters and the country would oppose such policy, and as for independence, he declared that no Englishman could be "either bold or Mad enough to presume to treat for the Mother Country on such a basis."[41]

But early in February 1778, after the British had already lost their best opportunity of getting a peace proposal to America before news of a French alliance arrived, the king urged Lord North to press forward with his conciliatory bills. George III was now convinced that war with France was imminent and hoped news of Britain's peace offer could be rushed to America.[42] But first North and his advisers had to draw up the terms to be offered the colonists.

The instructions and terms for the Carlisle Commission were prepared under considerably different circumstances than previous offers, and naturally reveal some changes in the government's attitude toward the Americans. The question of submission as a condition of negotiation was not central this time, but it was replaced by the assumption that Americans would accept a "return to their condition in 1763" as the "principle of the present negotiation," and therefore "that proposition, in general terms, must be agreed to at once."[43] It staggers the imagination that a British ministry could still harbor such a massive illusion after almost three years of warfare with the colonies, proclamation of the Declaration of Independence, extensive American negotiations with foreign powers, and the establishment of government based on popular consent. But if it is recalled that the British government and people were committed to a system whose primary constitutional doctrine was the authority of Parliament, and which made the first concern of its king and ministers the maintenance of the constitution wherever British dominion extended, then it is not so staggering a proposition. The structure of British politics and ideas severely limited the options available. Indeed, "the King, his ministers, and their supporters, both in and outside of Parliament, as well as those opposed to them, were alike the prisoners of certain fixed patterns of statecraft evolved during the past centuries."[44]

But if the Americans did agree to negotiate they would learn that Britain had repealed the tea tax, and that Parliament had given up its right to tax, in place of which England hoped for contributions as a "mere act of free will." Even the Declaratory Act could be superseded by a declaration of British and American rights that would be written into the treaty. Assurances would be given on the sanctity of American charters, governors could be elected, and no standing armies would be kept in the colonies during peace time. The British commissioners could consent to a permanent assembly such as Congress, and could even consider seats in Parliament for Americans, subject to referral to that body. It would not be necessary "to insist on a formal revocation" of the Declaration of Independence because this and other "votes, orders and resolutions, not being legal acts, will be in effect rescinded by the conclusion of the treaty."[45]

Such a list of concessions is impressive, and it is possible that these, if offered before the Declaration of Independence, might have satisfied the Americans and become the basis for a new imperial constitution. There is, of course, no way of proving this, and it may be that the real significance is that these terms were *not* offered before 1776. But a number of reputable historians have been impressed with this offer, and one has even suggested that the British government's ability to make

31

such an offer shows British statemanship in the eighteenth-century was not as bankrupt as frequently charged.[46]

The fact remains, however, that it took the shock of Saratoga and the threat of war with France to produce these concessions, and it is also true that the ministry gave a higher priority to its military plan changes than it did to getting its commissioners to America with its peace proposals. By the time the envoys arrived the French alliance had been agreed to, and the British army was in process of evacuating Philadelphia.[47] The peace offer of 1778, like previous offers, and for partly the same reasons, was foredoomed to failure.

Those who see the genesis of a federal empire in the offer of 1778 should recall its premise that the Americans still sought a return to the conditions of 1763. Further, they should notice that while the Carlisle Commission was authorized to consider making Congress a permanent body, its instructions also warned that "the sovereignty of the mother country should not be infringed [by the Congress] nor any powers given or ascribed to it that should be capable of being construed into an impeachment of the sovereign rights of His Majesty, and the constitutional control of this country."[48] In its instructions to the Carlisle Commission the government went as far as any British ministry of the day could dare—but as Bernard Bailyn accurately suggests, "to endorse, though still not in theory, the position that John Dickinson had advanced so long ago in the *Farmers Letters* .... was by then grotesquely irrelevant to the realities of the situation."[49]

An analysis and evaluation of the North ministry and its conciliatory efforts during the War of the Revolution supports the view that the "spectrum of possibilities" was slight.[50] It also confirms the belief that the British government operated from premises on which there was widespread agreement both in and outside of Parliament, and when the Americans challenged one of the fundamental political beliefs of the British nation—that of parliamentary supremacy—this consensus on basic principles not only prevented the ministers from considering real constitutional change, it also prevented them from appreciating the strength of the Americans and their depth of conviction.[51] That a conciliatory offer the Americans would take seriously could be developed from such a political and intellectual base was an impossible dream.

## NOTES

1. Benjamin Franklin to Joseph Galloway, 9 Jan. 1769, *The Papers of Benjamin Franklin*, ed. William B. Willcox (New Haven: Yale Univ. Press, 1972), XVI, 10-18.

2. The fullest discussion of the various conciliatory efforts during the Revolution is Weldon A. Brown, *Empire or Independence: A Study in the Failure of Reconciliation, 1774-1783* (Baton Rouge: Louisiana State Univ. Press, 1941).

3. Examples of this are, in varying degree: Esmond Wright, *Fabric of Freedom, 1763-1800* (New York: Hill and Wang, 1961), p. 70; Marshall Smelser, *The Winning of Independence* (New York: New Viewpoints, 1973), p. 20; Edmund S. Morgan, "The American Revolution: Revisionists in Need of Revising," *William and Mary Quarterly*, 3rd ser., 14 (Jan. 1957), 12; Benjamin W. Labaree, *The Boston Tea Party* (New York: Oxford Univ. Press, 1964), p. 264; Bernhard Knollenberg, *Origin of the American Revolution, 1759-1766* (New York: Macmillan, 1960), p. 5.

4. Carl Cone's remark on Burke is of interest here: "Those who see Burke as a spiritual father of the Commonwealth do not appreciate the sharp limits he placed in 1775 upon colonial autonomy. Burke believed in parliamentary supremacy, in all cases in the abstract, in all cases except taxation in practice." Carl B. Cone, *Burke and the Nature of Politics: the Age of the American Revolution* (Lexington: Univ. of Kentucky Press, 1957), p. 283. John C. Miller, *Origins of the American Revolution* (Boston: Atlantic, Little-Brown, 1943), pp. 223-24, points out that none of the Whig Opposition, Burke, Chatham, Shelburne, Camden, approved of imperial federation. Finally, it was Sir Lewis Namier's opinion, *England in the Age of the American Revolution*, p. 39, that "Burke and his friends, if in power" could not have saved the British Empire.

5. Sir Lewis Namier, *England in the Age of the American Revolution* (New York: St. Martin's Press, 1966 rev. ed.), p. 37.

6. See Jack M. Sosin, *Agents and Merchants: British Colonial Policy and the Origins of the American Revolution, 1763-1775* (Lincoln: Univ. of Nebraska Press, 1965), xiii-xiv. The concluding chapter of this book is a good summary of the British government's position in 1775.

7. George III to Lord North, 4 Feb. 1774, in Sir John Fortescue, ed., *The Correspondence of King George III from 1760 to December 1783* (6 vols., London: Macmillan, 1925-28), III, 59.

8. Quoted from the Dartmouth MSS by Bernard Donoughue, *British Politics and the American Revolution: the Path to War, 1773-75* (London: St. Martin's, 1964), p. 34.

9. For an interesting analysis of the ministry's actions here see Jack M. Sosin, "The Massachusetts Acts of 1774: Coercive or Preventive?" *Huntington Library Quarterly*, 26 (May 1963), 235-52; also, *Agents and Merchants*, pp. 185-87, for the ministry's rationale. The most recent study of the Coercive Acts is David Ammerman, *In the Common Cause: American Response to the Coercive Acts of 1774* (New York: Norton, 1975).

10. Lord Dartmouth's reaction and his remarks to Reed are quoted in Bradley D. Bargar, *Lord Dartmouth and the American Revolution* (Columbia: Univ. of South Carolina Press, 1965), pp. 105-09.

11. A summation and references on this point are in Ira D. Gruber, *The Howe Brothers and the American Revolution* (New York: Atheneum, 1972), pp. 39-42; see also Paul H. Smith, *Loyalists and Redcoats: A Study in British Revolutionary Policy* (Chapel Hill: Univ. of North Carolina Press, 1964), p. 10. By mid-September 1774, General Gage was warning the ministry against overconfidence but without effect; see Bernhard Knollenberg, *Growth of the American Revolution, 1766-1775* (New York: Macmillan, 1975), p. 168.

12. George III to Lord North, 11 Sept. 1774, Fortescue, III, 130-31.

13. There was, of course, opposition both inside and out of Parliament, but politically and realistically this was of no real help to the Americans; see Donoughue, *British Politics*, pp. 127-61.

14. Knollenberg, *Growth of the American Revolution*, p. 169. On the election of 1774 see Donoughue, *British Politics*, pp. 177-200.

15. George III to Lord North, 18 Nov. 1774, Fortescue, III, 153-54. To the suggestion by Dartmouth and John Pownall, that commissioners be sent to America, the king was negative because he felt this might show weakness; Great Britain, Historical Manuscripts Commission, *Report on the Manuscripts in Various Collections: the Manuscripts of Captain H. V. Knox* (6 vols., London, 1901-1909), VI, 258; George III to Lord North, 15 December 1774, Fortescue, III, 156.

16. According to Lord Suffolk, Gage was "too far gone to be recovered," Suffolk to Dartmouth, as quoted in Donoughue, *British Politics*, p. 212, and see also pp. 211, 217. Solicitor General Alexander Wedderburn was also highly critical of the British command in America; see Wedderburn to North, July 1775, Great Britain, Historical Manuscripts Commission, *Report on the Manuscripts of the Marquis of Abergavenny*, Tenth Report, Appendix, Part VI (London, 1887), p. 9; William Eden was severe in condemnation of Admiral Graves; see Eden to Lord George Germain, 3 Oct. 1775, Germain Papers, Clements Library, University of Michigan.

17. For the quote see J. Steven Watson, *The Reign of George III* (Oxford: Clarendon, 1960), p. 260; also Donoughue, *British Politics*, pp. 148-51, and Sosin, *Agents and Merchants*, pp. 199, 218 on the decline of mercantile support for the Americans.

18. *Ibid.*, pp. 190-26, for a fine summary of the failure of the colonial agents, and for the quote see Richard W. Van Alstyne, *Empire and Independence* (New York: Wiley, 1965), p. 34, quoting William Knox. Despite the Hutchinson letters affair Franklin was sought out by Dartmouth, and through David Barclay and Dr. John Fothergill an extensive series of discussions with Franklin were held in the period from December 1774 to February 1775. These sessions included games of chess with Mrs. Caroline Howe and conversations with her brother, Admiral Richard, Lord Howe. Franklin's "Hints" were forwarded to the ministry, but the negotiations foundered on the point of parliamentary supremacy. Franklin's own account is in his long letter to his son, William, 22 March 1775, found in Francis Wharton, ed., *The Revolutionary Diplomatic Correspondence of the United States* (6 vols., Washington, D.C., Govt. Printing Office, 1889), II, 6-58. An accurate and balanced account of these negotiations is in Sosin, *Agents and Merchants*, pp. 207-15.

19. Knollenberg, *Growth of the American Revolution*, p. 170, and Clarence E. Carter, comp. and ed., *The Correspondence of General Thomas Gage with the Secretaries of State and with the War Office and the Treasury 1763-1775* (2 vols., 1931-33, New Haven: Yale Univ. Press, reprint ed. 1969), I, 380, Gage to Dartmouth, 30 October 1774.

20. Donoughue, *British Politics*, pp. 220-24.

21. Dartmouth to Gage, 22 February 1775, Carter, ed., *Gage Correspondence*, II, 185.

22. Lord North always regarded British policy in this respect. See the long letter he had William Eden write Lord George Germain, 3 October 1775, Germain Papers, Clements Library, University of Michigan. North later (1778) claimed he had always intended to settle the American issue on the basis of conciliation and compromise, but held that victory was the proper moment to offer concessions, Thomas C. Hansard, comp., *The Parliamentary History of England from the Earliest Period to the Year 1803* (36 vols., London, 1806-1820), XIX, 765-66.

23. For a discussion of Chatham's plan of conciliation, as well as Lord North's bill, see Lawrence Henry Gipson, *The British Empire Before the American Revolution*, Vol. XII: *The Triumphant Empire: Britain Sails into the Storm, 1770-1776* (New York: Knopf, 1965), pp. 277-97. North's bill, with debates, introduced on 20 February and passed on 27 February, may be followed in *Parl. Hist.*, XVIII, 319-23.

24. Discussions of North's bill and the debates surrounding its introduction and passage are in the following: Brown, *Empire or Independence*, pp. 43-57; B. D. Bargar, *Lord Dartmouth*, pp. 140-42; Ira D. Gruber, *The Howe Brothers*, pp. 18-19. George H. Guttridge, *English Whiggism and the American Revolution* (Berkeley: Univ. of California Press, 1963, 2nd ed.), pp. 79-80, states that North was impolitic in

his presentation, and thereby insured suspicion as to his motives.

25. John R. Alden, *A History of the American Revolution* (New York: Knopf, 1969), p. 169. Lord Dartmouth sent a circular letter, dated 3 March 1775, with a copy of North's proposal to the colonial governors; see Benjamin F. Stevens, comp., *Stevens' Facsimiles of Manuscripts in European Archives Relating to America, 1773-1783* (25 vols., London, 1889-98), No. 1201.

26. Lord North to George III, [19 Feb. 1775], Fortescue, III, 176-77.

27. Franklin to William Franklin, 22 March 1775, Wharton, *Revolutionary Diplomatic Correspondence*, II, 54.

28. Gruber, *The Howe Brothers*, p. 19; Brown, *Empire or Independence*, p. 45; and Knollenberg, *Growth of the American Revolution*, pp. 172-73, sees the resolution as probably insincere; Edmund S. Morgan, *The Birth of the Republic* (Chicago: Univ. of Chicago Press, 1956), p. 69, dismisses the North plan as a "futile aside". On the other hand, Sosin, *Agents and Merchants*, p. 205; Van Alstyne, *Empire and Independence*, pp. 61-62; and Guttridge, *English Whiggism*, pp. 79-80, all see the proposal as sincere. North himself recalled (1778) that his 1775 proposal had been misrepresented and "made to appear so obscure as to go damned to America: so that Congress conceived, or took occasion to represent it as a scheme for showing divisions, and introducing taxation among them . . . .", *Parl. Hist.*, XIX, 762.

29. It should be recalled that by this time the Americans were firmly resolved to resist parliamentary sovereignty, as noted by William Smith, Jr., who believed the constitutional impasse was caused by "intellectual rigidity among leaders on both sides...", Robert M. Calhoon, "William Smith, Jr.'s Alternative to the American Revolution," *William and Mary Quarterly*, Ser. 3, 22 (Jan. 1965), p. 111.

30. Worthington C. Ford and Gaillard Hunt, eds., *Journals of the Continental Congress, 1774-1789* (34 vols., Washington: Govt. Printing Office, 1904-22), II, 155-62, for the petition to the king and the "Declaration on Taking Arms"; also Edmund C. Burnett, *The Continental Congress* (New York: Macmillan, 1941), pp. 71, 85-87 for discussion of these topics.

31. A draft of the Royal Proclamation of Rebellion is in *Stevens' Facsimiles*, No. 459.

32. See Gruber, *The Howe Brothers*, pp. 27-37, for details and a summary of these developments.

33. Charles R. Ritcheson, *British Politics and the American Revolution* (Norman: Univ. of Oklahoma Press, 1954), p. 203; Gerald S. Brown, *The American Secretary, The Colonial Policy of Lord George Germain, 1775-1778* (Ann Arbor: Univ. of Michigan Press, 1963), p. 67; Gruber, *The Howe Brothers*, pp. 72-79.

34. Ritcheson, *British Politics*, pp. 202-07; Brown, *American Secretary*, pp. 63-72; William Knox Memorandum, "Account of the

First Peace Commission of 1776," Knox Papers, X, 10, Clements Library, University of Michigan. This is incompletely calendared in Hist. MSS Comm., *Var. Coll.*, VI, 258-60.

35. William Eden to Lord North, [? October 1775], Br. Mus. Add. MSS 34412, ff. 369-70 (microfilm). This letter is also *Stevens' Facsimiles,* No. 345, but is misdated January 1778. Eden was discussing the conciliation plan of 1776, not 1778, and a reference to Admiral Shuldham's departure puts the date before 22 October. The key phrase Eden relates to North is Lord Mansfield's fear that "neither our Force nor the Exertion of it will be equal to the Magnitude and Exigency of Affairs."

36. The problem of submission as part of the Howes' instructions is discussed in: Ritcheson, *British Politics*, pp. 203-04; Brown, *American Secretary*, pp. 65-67; Gruber, *The Howe Brothers*, pp. 73-74; and for the phrase quoted here, William Knox, "Account of the First Peace Commission," Knox Papers, Clements Library.

37. The best account of the problems with Admiral Howe is in Gruber, *The Howe Brothers*, pp. 67-69; see also Ritcheson, *British Politics*, p. 202.

38. Ritcheson, *British Politics*, p. 207. It is of interest that the ministry excluded Rhode Island and Connecticut from the general peace terms until their governments had been altered to include appointed governors, among other changes. Lord Howe did win a minor concession from Germain on this point, but the whole episode is revealing in terms of the ministry's fixation on what it considered essential for negotiations with the colonies. For details see Brown, *American Secretary*, pp. 68-72.

39. Gruber, *The Howe Brothers*, pp. 38-39, 87.

40. North to William Eden, 4 Nov. 1777, Br. Mus. Add. MSS 34414, ff. 309-10. North was discussing the drafting of the king's speech, and his mood is further shown by his concluding sentence: "My idea of American affairs is, that if our success is as great as the most sanguine politician wishes or believes, the best use we can make of it is to get out of the dispute as soon as possible."

41. The government's reaction to Saratoga is briefly discussed in Alan S. Brown, "The British Peace Offer of 1778: A Study in Ministerial Confusion," *Papers of the Michigan Academy of Science, Arts, and Letters*, 40 (1955), 250-51; George III to Lord North, 13 January 1778, Fortescue, IV, 14-15.

42. George III to Lord North, February 2 and 9, 1778, Fortescue, IV, 33, 36.

43. Royal Instructions to the Peace Commission of 1778, printed in S. E. Morison, ed., *Sources and Documents Illustrating the American Revolution, 1764-1788* (Oxford: Clarendon, 1962, 2nd ed.), pp. 186-203,

quoting p. 192. *Stevens' Facsimiles*, No. 440, also reproduces the instructions.

44. Lawrence Henry Gipson, *The British Empire Before the American Revolution: Britain Sails into the Storm, 1770-1776*, XII, 269.

45. "Royal Instructions," Morison, *Documents*, pp. 186-203.

46. Vincent T. Harlow, *The Founding of the Second British Empire, 1763-1793:* Vol. I: *Discovery and Revolution* (London: Longmans, Green, 1952), p. 501; Ritcheson, *British Politics*, p. 258, sees the Carlisle Commission as introducing a "new concept of empire," a view not shared by this writer.

47. Military planning is discussed in William Bradford Willcox, "British Strategy in America in 1778," *Journal of Modern History*, 19 (1947), 97-121; also see Alan S. Brown, "British Peace Offer of 1778," pp. 254-60.

48. "Royal Instructions," Morison, *Documents*, p. 200.

49. Bernard Bailyn, *The Ideological Origins of the American Revolution* (Cambridge: Harvard Univ. Press, 1967), p. 227.

50. The phrase is from John Shy, "Thomas Pownall, Henry Ellis, and the Spectrum of Possibilities, 1763-1775," in Alison G. Olson and Richard M. Brown, eds., *Anglo-American Political Relations, 1675-1775* (New Brunswick: Rutgers Univ. Press, 1970). This excellent essay was useful in preparation of the present paper.

51. My conclusions here are reinforced by Jack P. Greene, "The Plunge of Lemmings: A Consideration of Recent Writings on British Politics and the American Revolution," *South Atlantic Quarterly*, 67 (1968), 170. Greene's remarks on several works discussed in the essay were extremely suggestive and helpful for this paper.

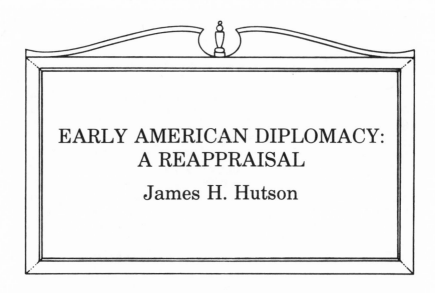

# EARLY AMERICAN DIPLOMACY: A REAPPRAISAL

## James H. Hutson

In 1961 Felix Gilbert published his influential *To the Farewell Address; Ideas of Early American Foreign Policy*. Unlike Corwin, Bemis, and other authorities on early American diplomacy, Gilbert was not primarily concerned with the diplomatic process, with the parry and thrust of negotiators. Rather, he explored the ideas which guided, and the presuppositions which underlay, early American diplomacy. In addition, he attempted to place early American diplomacy in the context of American diplomatic history as a whole. Finally, he offered a theory about the relationship of early American diplomacy to the American Revolutionary experience. His ambitious efforts — and misconceptions — will furnish the point of departure for this paper.[1]

Gilbert wrote his book during a period when American diplomacy was being scored by a group of writers, led by Hans J. Morgenthau, who claimed that its irresponsible oscillations between Wilsonian "idealistic internationalism" and isolationism helped to cause the Second World War. Morgenthau and his circle advocated a "realistic" approach to foreign policy—a recognition that politics

This article appeared in the *Quarterly Journal of the Library of Congress*, 33 (July 1976), 183-98. Reprinted by permission of the author.

among nations was an amoral struggle for power and that a country should calculate its goals accordingly. The Founding Fathers, they claimed, perceived this truth and practiced upon it, but succeeding generations of American statesmen were represented as benightedly straying into either isolationism or idealistic internationalism.[2]

What was the origin of these two concepts? Gilbert argued that they were present in tandem in the American mentality as far back as the settlement of the North American continent and that they quite naturally emerged as guiding principles of the diplomacy of the United States in 1776. But, he continued, experience in the world soon tempered the initial American idealism and by the time of George Washington's inauguration the American government was, as Morgenthau claimed, in the hands of men—the foremost being Alexander Hamilton—who approached the world realistically, although they did not entirely renounce idealism. Thus, Gilbert asserts, by the Federalist era "the basic issue of the American attitude toward foreign policy" was "the tension between Idealism and Realism."[3]

The most provocative feature of Gilbert's book is implicit and was, perhaps, unintended: the consideration of early American diplomacy as an aspect of the American Revolutionary process. Gilbert's interpretation of our early diplomacy seems to be an application to foreign affairs of the Progressive interpretation of the American Revolutionary period, the paradigm developed in the 1920s and 1930s by Charles Beard and others. The Progressive historians held that American independence was achieved by a group of liberal, even radical, leaders who displaced a conservative colonial elite; these liberal idealists were, in turn, swept aside by a conservative counterrevolution that produced the Constitution and embodied itself in the predominant Federalist party of the 1790s; the original goals and spirit of the Revolution were vindicated and restored, however, in 1801 with the election of the liberal champion, Thomas Jefferson. An idealistic, internationalistic foreign policy of 1776 being replaced by a hardheaded Hamiltonian realism of 1789 is nothing less than a Progressive interpretation of American foreign policy. When Gilbert's thesis is rounded off with a study of the administration of Thomas Jefferson, as is expertly done by Paul Varg, the evidence of Progressivism is even stronger: "The determination to approach foreign relations in terms of the ideal rather than in terms of existing realities predominated during the Revolution, lost much of its hold during the Washington administrations, and regained prominence with the election of Thomas Jefferson."[4] Not the least of the questions we should ask is whether a Progressive interpretation of early American diplomacy can stand up under scrutiny.

The most novel feature of Gilbert's thesis is his contention that American foreign policy, as it was conceived in 1776 and articulated in the famous Model Treaty of that year, presented two faces to the world: isolationism and idealistic internationalism. The desire of American statesmen to avoid entanglement in the wars and politics of Europe and to confine their country's relationship to Europe to commerce, free to all nations, has long been considered isolationism and nothing more. But Gilbert contends that these aspirations were also "idealistic and internationalistic."[5] His evidence is the alleged influence of the philosophes on the American Revolutionary generation. The foreign policy objectives of both the philosophes and the Americans were peace and free trade, Gilbert argues, and, therefore, he believes that Americans must have shared the philosophes' desire to bring about, through free trade, a "new age of peace" in which "relations between nations would become purely commercial contacts, and the need for a political diplomacy with alliances and balance of power would disappear from the international scene." Americans in 1776, in other words, must have been idealistic and internationalistic as well as isolationistic.[6]

42

Since historians of the American Revolution have never ascribed much influence to the philosophes, Gilbert's thesis, unsupported as it is by any evidence from the 1770s, would seem to be suspect on its face. In the past decade we have had, moreover, an authoritative investigation of the ideas behind the American Revolution by Bernard Bailyn, who has concluded that the mentality of the American Revolutionary leaders was formed principally by English Opposition writers.[7] Nowhere in his delineation of the intellectual sources of the Revolution does Bailyn so much as mention the French philosophes.[8] There is also contemporary testimony about the absence of the philosophes' influence in Revolutionary America. In his *Notes on the State of Virginia*, written in 1781-82, Thomas Jefferson conceded that French thinkers were virtually unknown in America: "we are but just becoming acquainted with her [France]," Jefferson wrote.[9] More important for our purposes is John Adams, the draftsman of the Model Treaty of 1776. Gilbert called Adams "the chief architect of the Model Treaty";[10] Adams regarded himself as the architect of the whole of early American foreign policy, the man who "'refin'd it first and show'd its use,' as really as Dean Swift did irony."[11] Therefore, Adams's scorn for the French philosophers is especially significant. Their system, he wrote Benjamin Rush on 22 December 1806, "I took some pains, more than five and twenty years ago, to understand; but could not find one Gentleman among the Statesmen, Philosophers, and Men of Letters, who pretended to understand it. I procured the Books of Quanay [Quesnay] and I could not understand much of them, and much of what I understood I did not believe. . . ."[12] The utter lack of influence of the philosophes on Adams is demonstrated by the reply he gave a friend in 1777 who was seeking to inform himself about political economy, about commerce and money in particular. Read Locke, Postlethwait, and Newton, Adams advised him.[13]

To see if there was at least a scintilla of support for

Gilbert's thesis about the influence of the philosophes, I examined every letter from the year 1776 in the files of the editorial office of the *Letters of Delegates to Congress, 1774-1789.* The editors of the letters, in one of the Library of Congress projects to celebrate the Bicentennial of the American Revolution, have attempted to collect every extant letter written by members of Congress before 1789. Nowhere in the letters of 1776 is there a mention of the philosophes, nor is there the slightest indication that any member regarded American foreign policy as ushering in a new era in which power politics would be abolished by the magic of free trade, and peace and goodwill would reign among men. The notion, then, that American foreign policy, as conceived in 1776, was given an idealistic, internationalistic cast by the philosophes is a myth.

It seems possible that Gilbert assumed that the American Revolutionary leaders were under the influence of the philosophes because he mistook what the Americans meant by "free trade," the panacea of the philosophes. This nostrum, as the philosophes concocted it, prescribed the complete elimination of tariffs, duties, exclusions, and monopolies. Trade would be as free as air; each nation would specialize in the production of that which nature enabled it to do best and would exchange its products with its neighbors for the benefit of all. Such a vision inspired few Americans in 1776, for the emancipation of commerce was not a goal of their Revolution. Quite the contrary, Americans willingly accepted the British mercantilist system under which they had prospered and were content to continue living within its confines. "We cheerfully consent the operation of such acts [i.e., the Navigation Acts] of the British parliament," declared the First Continental Congress in October 1774, "as are bona fide, restrained to the regulation of our external commerce, for the purpose of securing the commercial advantages of the whole empire to the mother country. . . ."[14] "It has been said," the Second Continental

Congress advised the British people in July 1775, "that we refuse to submit to the Restrictions on our Commerce. From whence is this Inference drawn? Not from our Words, we have repeatedly declared the Contrary; and we again profess our Submission to the several Acts of Trade and Navigation passed before the Year 1763. . . ."[15] When John Adams drafted the Model Treaty in the summer of 1776, did he suddenly depart from these sentiments? Not at all, although a superficial reading of the Model Treaty has persuaded many that it was a charter for free trade.[16]

The Model Treaty proposed commercial reciprocity rather than commercial freedom. It stated that the United States, in its ports, would treat subjects of a foreign power as it treated its own citizens, if the foreign power would do the same for American citizens in its ports. A foreigner trading to an American port would encounter no restraints at the customs house. American leaders, presiding over a predominantly agrarian nation, perceived it to be contrary to the country's interests to lay import duties which would raise prices to the farmer. But just because foreign merchants would pay no duties in the United States, Americans did not expect to be exempt from duties in foreign ports. The objective of the Model Treaty was not to immunize American traders against duties, but to assure that foreign governments did not discriminate against them in favor of their own citizens. In insisting that Americans be treated as Britishers in British ports, the Model Treaty in fact accepted the Navigation Acts, for Americans would be bound by the whole system of "enumerated" quantities, prohibitory duties, and all the other appurtenances of mercantilism (as they would be by the national mercantilistic system in French, Spanish, and other European ports). What the Model Treaty aimed for was the maintenance of the American carrying trade, as it had been enjoyed under the British Navigation Acts. This becomes clear from a statement of John Adams to Robert Livingston in May 1783, when a preliminary peace, but not a commercial

45

treaty, had been concluded with Britain. "The idea of reviving trade, upon the plan of the laws of Great Britain before the war . . . might be admissible," Adams wrote, until a treaty could be settled.[17]

But Great Britain refused to grant a commercial treaty to the United States. American statesmen responded, not by turning the other cheek and attempting to disarm British hostility with free trade, but with projects of countervailing navigation acts, excluding British shipping from American ports.[18] Thomas Jefferson himself— who in the late 1780s, under the spell of the French intellectual world as ambassador to Versailles, made a handful of statements which seemed to support free trade—"helped to draft the congressional address of April 30, 1784, recommending that the states 'vest Congress with so much power over their commerce . . . to enable them . . . to pass something like the British navigation act.'"[19] And it was Jefferson's partisans, led by Madison, who fought in Congress throughout the 1790s for a system of discriminatory commercial duties.[20] The notion that American leaders were committed to free trade, as the philosophes understood it, is therefore an error.

The consensus among American leaders, in fact, seems to have been that an unrestricted exchange of goods with foreign nations was among the greatest potential threats to the Revolutionary experiment in free government. Recent writers have argued that the principal objective of the American Revolutionary leaders, which both domestic and foreign policy were designed to serve, was the establishment and preservation of a republic. A republic was a concept of eighteenth-century political scientists, who believed that there were exact conditions which assured its health: existence in a circumscribed area, absence of a standing military establishment, and, pre- eminently, the presence of virtue in the people at large. Virtue was understood in a civic sense, as a passion for the public good. Its antithesis, as well as the chief threat to republican government, was luxury, which was believed to breed corruption. Luxury was understood as conspicuous consumption to which one became so addicted that he fell into the power of—was corrupted by—those who could supply the means to maintain the habit.

The principal purveyor of luxury in American society, the Revolutionary leaders believed, was foreign commerce, and they condemned it unsparingly.[21] "Commerce produces money, money Luxury and all three are incompatible with Republicanism," wrote John Adams, epitomizing American thinking on the matter.[22] No less representative was Thomas Paine's statement in *Common Sense* that "'Commerce diminishes the spirit both of patriotism and military defense' and would eventually destroy America's soul."[23] John Adams, in fact, declaimed almost nonstop against commerce. "The Spirit of Commerce," he wrote Mercy Warren on 16 April 1776, "Corrupts the morals of families as well as destroys their Happiness, it is much to be feared [it] is incompatible with that purity of Heart and Greatness of Soul which is necessary for a happy Republic."[24] "We must guard," he wrote Mercy's husband, James, on 15 December 1782, against "that excessive Influx of Commerce Luxury and Inhabitants from abroad, which will soon embarrass Us."[25] "The Intelligent advocate of Liberty," Adams informed Elbridge Gerry on 25 April 1785, is always against "the Commercial Spirit and innumerable other evil Spirits."[26]

It was not just Adams and men of his type who feared the corrosive effects of commerce. Merchants themselves were apprehensive about it. Tristram Dalton, for example, agreed with those who argued "against an extensive trade, as ruinous to the managers of a Republic."[27] And Silas Deane, the tragic symbol of the Revolutionary merchant, shared the common sentiments about trade: only "by banishing wealth and luxury, and holding commerce, the parent of both, in abhorrence" would it be possible, he contended, to preserve republican government.[28] Curiously enough, the very philosophes—Mably, Mirabeau, Raynal—whom Gilbert quotes as expecting free trade to produce a regenerate world order were warning Americans in the 1780s about the incompatibility of commerce and republican government.[29] Mably was particularly shrill about the baleful effects of trade, stating that "I cannot avoid coinciding with the opinion of Plato, who, in order to secure the welfare of a republic, recommended that it should not establish itself either near the sea, nor upon the borders of any large river."[30]

What antidotes were available to the poison of unbridled commerce? One was suggested by Pennsylvania Congressman James Searle, who in 1781 asserted "that commerce had injured us, that the merchants of America were, without example, such vile rogues and speculators that it would be happy for America if they were instantly extirpated. . . ."[31] Most American leaders, however, preferred to extirpate foreign trade rather than those who participated in it. Jefferson's assertion that "it might be better for us to abandon the ocean altogether" and his wish that "there were an ocean of fire between us and the old world" were characteristic of a broad band of American opinion.[32] As David Rittenhouse put it: let nature "raise her everlasting bars between the new and old world . . . and make a voyage to Europe as impracticable as one to the moon."[33] John Adams expressed the matter this way: "If all Intercourse between Europe and America could be cut off, forever, if every ship we have were burnt, and the keel of another never to be laid, we might still be the happiest people upon earth, and in fifty years the most powerful. The Luxuries we import from Europe, instead of promoting our prosperity, only enfeeble our race of men & retard the increase of population."[34]

A corollary to this commerce-phobia was a movement which developed just after the conclusion of peace with Britain in 1783, to insulate America further from Europe by sending no diplomatic representatives to the Old World. Europeans would then have no justification for contaminating the United States by sending their diplomats here. "I can see no necessity but great inconveniences in sending Ministers abroad and receiving them at home," wrote Elbridge Gerry to John Adams on 23 November 1783, "inconveniences of being entangled with European politics, of being the puppets of European Statesmen, of being gradually divested of our virtuous republican principles, of being a divided, influenced and dissipated people; of being induced to prefer the splendor of a court to the happiness of our citizens; and finally of changing our form of government for a vile Aristocracy or an arbitrary Monarchy."[35] One month later a committee of Congress, containing Gerry and Jefferson, reported that it would be "inconvenient at present . . . to keep ministers resident at the courts of Europe."[36] The desire to seal the country off completely from Europe in the interest of preserving republican purity shows that the ideal design of American Revolutionary leaders was not to use their foreign policy as an instrument to reform international politics, but to have no foreign policy at all, to move the country not toward idealistic internationalism but in the opposite direction, toward and indeed beyond isolationism to hermitry.

But such a design was "theory only," said Jefferson, "and a theory which the servants of America are not at liberty to follow. Our people have a decided taste for navigation and commerce . . . and their servants are in duty bound to calculate all their measures on this datum. . . ."[37] Or, as Adams put it, it was vain "to amuse ourselves with the thoughts of annihilating Commerce unless as Philosophical Speculations"; Americans were "as aquatic as the Tortoises and Sea Fowls" and "the love of Commerce with its Conveniences and pleasures" was a habit in them "as unalterable as their Natures."[38] Therefore, the leaders of the new republic never seriously tried to seal it off from other nations. The United States, they realized, must participate in the world and meet it on its own terms.

The world the American Revolutionary leaders found themselves in was a brutal, amoral cockpit. In the decade before American independence one of Europe's largest kingdoms—Poland—was divided by its neighbors; a government—Sweden—was overthrown by the machinations of its friends; a national liberation movement—in Corsica—was ruthlessly suppressed. A major war had ended in 1763 and another one was expected at any time. "There was something in the Minds of the English and French," wrote John Adams, "which impelled them irresistibly to War every Ten or fifteen Years."[39] No one in America expected international politics to improve. "Steeped in radical Whig pessimism," as Gordon Wood puts it, Americans believed Europe was beyond redemption.[40] This was a frame of mind which could not—and did not—support international reforming enterprises.

The world in which Americans found themselves was, above all, a world in which power was king. Perhaps nowhere does Gilbert err more egregiously than in stating that it was "difficult" for colonial Americans "to comprehend the importance of the power factor" in political relationships.[41] As Bailyn reconstructs American Revolutionary thought, he observes that "the acuteness of the colonists' sense" of power in politics is "one of the most striking things to be found" in it.[42] Bailyn stresses the colonists' consuming fear of power as a threat to liberty. But fear often generates respect, even admiration, and the Americans frequently congratulated themselves to the point of boasting about the power they collectively possessed, a habit the Loyalists found both foolish and offensive. "Ever since the reduction of Canada," wrote Thomas Chandler in 1774, "we have been bloated with a vain opinion of our own power and importance." "Intoxicated with their own importance," George Rome complained, the colonists were "growing more imperious, haughty, nay insolent every day."[43]

Consciousness of American power can be credited principally to the demographic discoveries of Benjamin Franklin in his *Observations Concerning the Increase of Mankind*, published in 1751. Long before Franklin wrote, however, folk wisdom had predicted that America would become the seat of world power. New Englanders believed that the Pilgrim Fathers had chiseled into Plymouth Rock the prophecy:

> The eastern nations sink, their glory ends
> And empire rises where the sun descends.

In 1807, John Adams remembered that there was nothing "more ancient in my memory than the observation that arts, sciences, and empire had travelled westward; and in conversation it was always added, since I was a child, that their next leap would be over the Atlantic into America."[44] Journeying through the colonies in 1759, Andrew Burnaby heard what Adams had heard: "An idea, strange as it is visionary, has entered into the minds of the generality of mankind, that empire is travelling westward." The colonists, he noted, were "looking forward with eager and impatient expectation to that destined moment when America is to give law to the rest of the world."[45]

Franklin's *Observations* supplied scientific confirmation for this expectation. By demonstrating that the population of the colonies was doubling approximately every twenty years and would continue to do so into the indefinite future, he showed how "America, an immense territory, favoured by Nature with all advantages of climate, soil, great navigable rivers, and lakes, &c. must become a great country, populous and mighty."[46] The impact of the *Observations* on young John Adams, as he read it in 1755, was duplicated every time the pamphlet was read in the colonies: "Soon after the reformation," Adams wrote, "a few people came over into this new world for conscience' sake. Perhaps this apparently trivial incident may transfer the great seat of empire into

America. It looks likely to me; . . . our people, according to the exactest computations, will in another century become more numerous than England itself. Should this be the case, since we have . . . all the naval stores of the nation in our hands, it will be easy to obtain the mastery of the seas; and then the united force of all Europe will not be able to subdue us."[47]

Not until 1776 did anything like a majority of Americans favor independence. Before that time, the phenomenon of rising American power was always considered within the context of the British Empire and of the mercantilistic thinking in which the empire was conceived. That the economic outlook of the American Revolutionary leaders was shaped principally by mercantilism—as William Appleman Williams, among others, has argued—is, I believe, indisputable. True, no American statesman favored the rigidly statist economy, designed to produce a favorable balance of trade as the highest national priority, which the champions of mercantilism prescribed. But almost all Americans subscribed to the mercantilist dogma that monetary wealth was power and that commerce was the parent of wealth and hence of power.

In his *Observations* Franklin made the connection between American population growth, British commerce, and British national power. Britain's commerce, he reasoned, would multiply in proportion as the consumers of her goods in America increased. It would double, in other words, every twenty years. "What an Accession of Power to the British Empire by Sea as well as Land" would result. "What Increase of Trade and Navigation! What Numbers of Ships and Seamen!"[48] Because of the magnitude of America's contribution to Britain's power, Franklin believed (as he wrote in 1760) that the "foundations of the future grandeur and stability of the British empire lie in America,"[49] a refrain which other American writers immediately picked up. "The Foundations of the Power and Glory of Great Britain are Based in America," claimed John Dickinson in 1765.[50] America, declared George Wythe in 1774, "is one of the Wings upon which the British Eagle has soared to the Skies."[51] The union of Britain with the American colonies had raised her, the Second Continental Congress affirmed, "to a power the most extraordinary the world had ever known."[52] "The commercial advantages Britain had enjoyed with the Colonies," declared the Committee of Secret Correspondence on 3 March 1776, "had contributed greatly to her late wealth and importance."[53] "The English," wrote John Adams on 4 August 1779, "by means of their commerce and extensive settlements abroad, arose to a degree of opulence and naval power" which had allowed them to tyrannize the world.[54]

These statements—and their like could be pyramided endlessly—demonstrate more than the mercantilistic slant of American thinking; they also show that in the years before independence Americans believed that, by raising Britain to the pinnacle of power she enjoyed as a result of the Seven Years' War, they were the key component in the European balance of power. As Robert Morris wrote: "From my knowledge of the Commerce of this Country with Europe I dare assert that whatever European Power possess the presumption of it, must of consequence become the richest and most potent in Europe."[55] American leaders believed, in fact, that if the connection between the colonies and Britain continued, the European balance of power would be annihilated in favor of total British hegemony. For the power of the British Empire would not, in the American view, be static. As American population relentlessly increased, so would the power of the empire. "Our trade was rapidly increasing with our increase of people, and in greater proportion," a committee of Congress declared in March 1776.[56] With these facts in mind, John Adams concluded that in another war the power of a united British Empire would have destroyed France's "existence as a maritime and commercial power," would have been "fatal" to her.[57]

Nor would, in Adams's opinion, the commerce and even the independence of the Netherlands have survived against an indivisible British Empire.[58] And the freedom of the seas, any place in the world, would have been an impossibility in the face of such a coalition.[59] On the other hand, Adams believed that for America, upon becoming independent, to deny her commerce to Britain would be "fatal" to the mother country, would "ruin" her, sentiments in which all of his colleagues agreed.[60] The kingdom, declared Richard Henry Lee at the First Continental Congress, "could not exist" without the commercial connection with America;[61] the dissolution of this connection, the Second Continental Congress informed the inhabitants of Great Britain, would "deliver you, weak and defenceless, to your natural Enemies,"[62] would reduce Great Britain, a correspondent of Franklin's predicted, "to a State of being a Province of France."[63] It was indisputable, then, to Adams and the other American leaders that the power the united colonies possessed made them the arbiter of the European balance of power. A "connection with America," Adams wrote Patrick Henry on 9 July 1778, "must in the future decide the Ballance of Maritime Power in Europe."[64]

Such a view was indistinguishable from that of the French foreign minister, Choiseul, who wrote in 1759 that "the true balance of power really resides in commerce and in America."[65] Choiseul was an exemplary practitioner of power politics, which, according to Gilbert, characterized European statecraft in the eighteenth century. "The eighteenth century," Gilbert writes, "was an era of 'pure politics' entirely dominated by the concept of power." The devotees of power politics, he continues, were "enthusiastic advocates" of the doctrines of the balance of power and the interests of states.[66] Although there is no evidence that Choiseul's ideas influenced the American Revolutionary leaders, they yielded nothing to him in the conviction with which they espoused the concepts of power politics. Foreign policy discussions in the Continental Congress were conducted in the vocabulary of the balance of power. "It is acknowledged *on all Hands*," wrote Elbridge Gerry on 11 November 1776, "that now is the Time for France & Spain to destroy the Balance of power which has been heretofore said to be preserved in Europe, but considered as preponderating against them."[67] The following passage from a letter of John Adams to James Warren, 20 March 1783, gives the terms in which foreign affairs were debated in the Continental Congress:

> Gentlemen can never be too often requested to recollect the Debates in Congress in the Years 1775 and 1776, when the Treaty with France was first in Contemplation. The Nature of those Connections, which ought to be formed between America and Europe, will never be better understood than they were at that time. It was then said, there is a Ballance of Power in Europe. Nature has formed it. Practice and Habit have confirmed it, and it must forever exist. It may be disturbed for a time, by the accidental Removal of a Weight from one Scale to the other; but there will be a continual Effort to restore the Equilibrium. . . . If We give exclusive priviledges in Trade, or form perpetual Alliances offensive and defensive with the Powers in one Scale, We infallibly make Enemies of those in the other. . . . Congress adopted these Principles and this System in its purity. . . ."[68]

Calculations about the interests of states were at least as frequent as speculations about gyrations in the balance of power. Wrote Adams in his diary on 1 March 1776: "How is the Interest of France and Spain affected, by the dispute between B. and the C[olonies]? Is it the Interest of France [to] stand neuter, to join with B. or to join with the C. Is it not her Interest, to dismember the B. Empire?"[69] Or, from the same pen: "No attachment between Nations arising merely from a Similarity of Laws and Government, is ever very strong or sufficient to bind Nations together who have opposite or even different Interests."[70] Finally, that other staple of power-political analysis — natural friends and natural enemies — was a constant presence in congressional discourse.[71]

Where did the Revolutionary leaders acquire these views, realistic enough and tough enough to please the most hardheaded of Morgenthau's disciples? The English Opposition writers may have been their source. Algernon Sidney, a great favorite of the Revolutionary generation, was an unabashed power politician.[72] Bolingbroke, whom John Adams held in high esteem, wrote copiously on the balance of power and is cited as an expert on the concept by modern historians.[73] Most other Opposition writers, however, were relatively silent on foreign affairs, their main concern being the preservation of public liberty from domestic threats. A specific source cannot easily be identified for American views; they seem rather to have reflected a belief common in the British Empire (championed by the Whigs, who represented it as being sanctioned by the Glorious Revolution), that it was Britain's interest to maintain a balance of power in Europe.[74] A conversation of John Adams's in France in 1778 speaks to this point. A Dutch merchant told him "that they in Holland had regarded England as the Bulwark of the Protestant Religion and the most important Weight in the Ballance of Power in Europe against France. I answered," Adams related, "that I had been educated from my Cradle in the same Opinion. . . ."[75]

American statesmen in 1776 approached foreign affairs as power politicians. They conceived the Model Treaty as an instrument to play the European balance of power for their own advantage. Freeing American trade from the British monopoly and giving France access to it would, Adams and his colleagues correctly calculated, bring Louis XVI to their support, because emancipating American trade would curb Britain's overweening power. "I knew," wrote Adams, "that France and Spain then dreaded the naval power of the United British Empire to such a degree that I thought it impossible they should let slip the opportunity of striking one pistol at least out of the hand of an enemy who constantly threatened them with two."[76] But Americans were determined not to exchange a British monopoly of their trade for a French one. Having fought, hated, and derided the French for as long as any of them could remember, Americans in 1776 simply could not refrain from regarding the subjects of the Most Christian King with fear and suspicion. As Carter Braxton put it, France was a nation "famous for Intrigue and Deception,"[77] sentiments which the successful wartime collaboration with Louis XVI failed to stanch. "Neither England nor America," wrote John Adams on 20 May 1783, "could depend upon the Moderation of such absolute Monarchies and such ambitious Nations" as France and Spain.[78] Perhaps John Dickinson best expressed the American attitude toward France in his speech of 1 July 1776, opposing the Declaration of Independence. "Suppose we shall ruin her [Great Britain]. France must rise on her Ruins. Her Ambition. Her Religion. Our Dangers from thence. We shall weep at our Victory."[79]

If American leaders in 1776 were apprehensive about the future behavior of France, they were certain Britain would be inimical toward them. On 1 July 1776, John Adams predicted that the war between Britain and America "would terminate in an incurable animosity between the two Countries." "They hate us, universally, from the throne to the footstool, and would annihilate us, if in their power," he wrote John Jay on 13 August 1782.[80] That the definitive treaty of 1783 left Canada in Britain's hands was regarded as particularly ominous by American leaders, for, as Hamilton declared in *The Federalist* no. 6, "it has . . . become a sort of axiom in politics, that vicinity, or nearness of situation, constitutes nations natural enemies."[81] Neighboring nations, asserted Edmund Randolph, "were bound to clash in 'bloodshed and slaughter.'"[82] In 1778 Richard Henry Lee predicted that "British possession of Canada, N. Sco. and the Floridas will inevitably produce" a "War in 7 years."[83] The seas, where Britain reigned as the imperious master, were also considered a point of certain friction. Since Americans would be engaging in sea-borne commerce, "wars then must sometimes be our lot," prophesied Jefferson.[84] Expecting trouble from Britain, Americans heeded Adams when, as minister to London from 1785 to 1788, he warned them that they should "keep up a constant Expectation of War," that Britain would "make war immediately against us" whenever an opportunity should arise.[85]

The world, as Americans in the Revolutionary era saw it, was like nothing which has appeared in American history except in certain years after the Second World War when the United States was simultaneously at sword's point with Russia and with China: the country was confronted at the same time with the enmity of two of the most powerful nations in the world, who were themselves implacable foes. The Revolutionary leaders responded to this situation by using their principal resource—commerce—to create a balance of power between their two antagonists, so that each would be able to restrain the aggressions of the other against the United States. That does not mean that in formulating the free trade provisions of the Model Treaty Adams and his colleagues expected to create an exact parity of power between Britain and France. If Britain availed herself of the terms offered by the Model Treaty, she would, Adams believed, obtain "more of American Trade . . . than France" and would derive from it "more support" for her navy than the French would. She would, he believed, "recover . . . much of her Commerce, and perhaps equal Consideration and Profit and Power from [America] as ever."[86] This was a remarkable policy since Britain was regarded as America's "natural Enemy for the future," who "would clean the wooden shoes of the French upon Condition that they would permit them to wreck their Vengeance on us."[87] Yet, conceding British enmity in its fullest measure, Adams considered it folly to enfeeble her vis-a-vis France. The United States, he contended, "ought with the utmost Firmness to resist every thought of giving to France any unequal advantage in our Trade even over England, for it never could be our Interest to ruin England, or annihilate their maritime Power, if we could possibly save our Liberty and independence without it."[88] And in 1783 Adams recalled that "in the years 1775 and 1776" he had "laid it down as a first principle that . . . above all . . . it could never be our interest to ruin Great Britain, or injure or weaken her any further than should be necessary to our independence and our alliance."[89] Why should Britain not be injured excessively? Because "the time might come," Benjamin Rush recalled Adams saying in 1776, "when we should be obliged to call upon Britain to defend us against France."[90] The draftsman of the Model Treaty did not see all of its benefits going to Britain, however. Giving France freedom to trade with the United States would extend her "navigation and Trade, augment her resources of naval Power . . . and place her on a more equal footing with England."[91] Thus strengthened, France would be better able to discourage British designs on America.

American Revolutionary leaders did not, however, place sole reliance on the operations of the balance of power to protect them. They firmly believed in what we today would call the doctrine of deterrence; that is, they believed that in the predatory world they inhabited the possession of power and the willingness to use it was a guarantor of peace. In other words, they subscribed to the ancient maxim: "si velis pacem, para bellum"—if you want peace, prepare for war. This, John Adams claimed in 1808, had been his system throughout his life.[92] It had been the system of his compatriots, too. Listen to Jefferson: "Whatever enables us to go to war, secures our peace"; "weakness provokes insult and injury, while a condition to punish it often prevents it."[93] To Washington: "If we desire to secure peace . . . it must be known, that we are at all times ready for War"; "to be prepared for

War is one of the most effectual means of preserving peace."[94] To Franklin: "The Way to secure Peace is to be prepared for War."[95] To Jay: "We should remember that to be constantly prepared for war is the only way to have peace."[96] To Henry; "A preparation for War is necessary to obtain peace."[97] To Marshall: "If we be prepared to defend ourselves, there will be little inducement to attack us."[98] To Gadsden: "The only Way to prevent the sword from being used is to have it ready."[99] And to Richard Henry Lee: "Our leaders [should] engrave upon their minds the wisdom of the inscription upon the arsenal of Berne in Switzerland—'That people happy are, who, during peace, are preparing the necessary stores for war.'"[100]

American leaders were not power hungry—at least not until Hamilton's military ambitions ran amok in the late 1790s. They believed an impressive military establishment was easily within their country's reach. John Adams, for example, wrote Jay in 1785 that if British commercial warfare forced the United States to adopt a navigation act in retaliation, America could, in ten years, have the third navy in the world. But why, he asked, would Britain force us "to try experiments against our own inclinations?"[101] He and his colleagues did not want a surfeit of military power, because they feared it would be fatal to the republican government they wished so desperately to maintain. The power they wanted was modest: adequate military supplies, well-disciplined militias in each state, and a middling naval force. This power, coupled with America's vast land mass and booming population, would, they felt, deter any potential enemy.

It is my contention—supported, I hope, by the documentation in this article—that a consensus existed among the leaders of the American Revolution about foreign policy in 1776 and endured through the adoption of the federal Constitution.[102] American leaders operated, in foreign politics, according to the assumptions of power politics that dominated contemporary European statecraft. They believed that the balance of power was "natural"—one of the magic words of the eighteenth century—and that it was their duty to manipulate it for their country's advantage. They also believed that, far from being ignoble, the possession of military power was justifiable and necessary, because it helped to preserve peace. A consensus on these principles does not allow for the possibility that at its inception American foreign policy was motivated by a crusading internationalistic idealism; equally inadmissible is a Progressive interpretation of early American foreign policy which sees an incipient liberalism of 1776 devoured by a conservative reaction in 1787, only to resurrect itself with Thomas Jefferson in 1801.

The consensus in foreign policy began to erode, I believe, when Citizen Genêt brought the passions of the French Revolution to American shores in 1793. Americans rushed to the standards of the principal belligerents, for some saw Britain, others France, embodying principles of government on which they thought their own welfare depended. Ideological partisanship became intense and overwhelmed the dispassionate temper essential for the conduct of a balance-of-power foreign policy. Hamilton in the late 1790s appeared to favor an outright alliance with Britain. Jefferson, on the other hand, was frequently so provoked with the British that he wished for their destruction: "down with England," he declared in 1807. Yet in their calmer moments both men, and their supporters as well, recognized the United States' interest in the preservation of the European balance of power. "I wish . . . that a salutary balance may be ever maintained," wrote Jefferson in 1815.[103]

After 1815, the commitment of American statesmen to balance of power politics disappeared for more than a century. The primary reason was that the dual threat Americans perceived from the two most powerful nations in Europe dissipated at the conclusion of the Napoleonic wars. France was prostrate. Britain was stronger than ever, but after what Americans called the War of 1812 a long and gradual warming of relations with the mother country set in, so that she was no longer perceived as a malign threat. Rather, her absolute control of the seas provided what has been called "free security" for the United States, a shield behind which the country grew virtually unmolested for a century. Some scholars have argued that the true, though hidden, reason the United States entered the First World War was to counteract the German Empire's threat to the European balance of power, but this thesis is difficult to substantiate. What is clear is that at the end of the Second World War the United States perceived itself to be threatened by the Soviet Union, augmented a few years later by its ally, the People's Republic of China. Thus, the world in the decades approaching the Bicentennial of the American Revolution appeared remarkably similar to the world into which the Founding Fathers introduced the United States as an independent nation. And the foreign policy which the United States has pursued since the end of the Second World War, based on the creation of a balance of power in Europe and on a sufficiency of military power in the nation's hands, is identical to that followed by the statesmen of the Revolutionary era. This is not to suggest that American foreign policy since 1945 has been inspired or instructed by the foreign policy of the Founding Fathers; there is no evidence whatever of such linkage. Rather the connection between the two eras is what the similitude of foreign policy reveals about an enduring trait in the American character: whenever confronted with a threat of force, Americans will respond with counterforce.

A balance of power foreign policy is not, then, some exotic malady inflicted upon the American people for the first time by the Cold War. It is as old as the Republic and bears the imprimatur of the Founding Fathers. A venerable policy, to be sure. But also a wise one? History will tell.

## NOTES

1. For the use of Gilbert by the most perceptive recent students of American diplomacy, see Paul A. Varg, *Foreign Policies of the Founding Fathers* (East Lansing: Michigan State Univ. Press, 1963), pp. 1-4; Merrill Peterson, "Thomas Jefferson and Commercial Policy, 1783-1793," *William and Mary Quarterly*, Ser. 3, 22 (October 1965), 588; William C. Stinchcombe, *The American Revolution and the French Alliance* (Syracuse: Syracuse Univ. Press, 1969), pp. 6-7; Gerald Stourzh, *Alexander Hamilton and the Idea of Republican Government* (Stanford: Stanford Univ. Press, 1970), pp. 146ff.; Lawrence S. Kaplan, *Colonies Into Nation: American Diplomacy, 1763-1801* (New York: Macmillan, 1972), pp. 91-94.

2. See Hans J. Morgenthau, *In Defense of the National Interest; a Critical Examination of American Foreign Policy* (New York: Alfred A. Knopf, 1951).

3. Felix Gilbert, *To the Farewell Address; Ideas of Early American Foreign Policy* (Princeton: Princeton Univ. Press, 1961), p. 136, also pp. 4-6, 72-73.

4. Varg, *Foreign Policies*, p. 4.

5. Gilbert, *To the Farewell Address*, p. 72.

6. Ibid., p. 69; see also chap. 3, especially pp. 56-69.

7. Bailyn's thesis is most fully developed in *The Ideological Origins of the American Revolution* (Cambridge: Belknap Press of Harvard Univ. Press, 1967).

8. Unless Montesquieu is to be considered a philosophe, of which there is considerable doubt. Stourzh claims that Montesquieu influenced early American foreign policy in an idealistic direction, but his description of Montesquieu's foreign policy ideas makes it appear that the Frenchman considered trade as a source of power, as did the mercantilists and other power politicians, at least as often as he did an instrument of international comity. Stourzh, *Hamilton and Republican Government*, pp. 140-48.

9. *Notes on the State of Virginia*, in *The Life and Selected Writings of Thomas Jefferson*, ed. Adrienne Koch and William Peden (New York: Random House, Modern Library, 1944), p. 215.

10. Gilbert, *To the Farewell Address*, p. 49.

11. Adams to Benjamin Rush, 30 September 1805, *The Spur of Fame; Dialogues of John Adams and Benjamin Rush, 1805-1813*, ed. John A. Schutz and Douglass Adair (San Marino, Calif.: Huntington Library, 1966), p. 39

12. Alexander Biddle, ed., *Old Family Letters*, 2 vols. (Philadelphia: Lippincott, 1892), 1: 120; see also Adams to John Jay, 26 February 1786, Adams Family Papers microfilm (Boston: Massachusetts Historical Society, 1954-), reel 112. Edward Handler observed that

before February 1778, when Adams embarked on his first European diplomatic mission, the ideas of the French Enlightenment "exerted minimum influence, whether by attraction or repulsion, on his mind." *America and Europe in the Political Thought of John Adams* (Cambridge: Harvard Univ. Press, 1964), p. 33. For substantiation of this point, see Zoltan Haraszti, *John Adams & the Prophets of Progress* (Cambridge: Harvard Univ. Press, 1952), p. 19.

13. To John Thaxter, 8 April 1777, Adams Papers microfilm, reel 91.

14. James H. Hutson, ed., *A Decent Respect to the Opinions of Mankind; Congressional State Papers, 1774-1776* (Washington: Library of Congress, 1975), p. 54.

15. Ibid., pp. 105-06. In January 1776 members of Congress, formulating proposals for reconciliation with Great Britain, pledged, on one occasion, that "the Navigation Act will remain inviolate" and, on another, that Americans would "confirm, if it be required, by perpetual Acts of their several Legislatures the Acts commonly called the Acts of Navigation." Lord Drummond's Minutes, 10-11 January 1776, and John Dickinson, "Proposed Instructions for Commissioners to Negotiate Peace with Great Britain," 9-24 January 1776; both documents in the editorial office of *Letters of Delegates to Congress, 1774-1789*, Library of Congress.

16. For the text of the Model Treaty, see U.S. Continental Congress, *Journals of the Continental Congress, 1774-1789*, ed. Worthington C. Ford et al., vol. 5 (Washington: Library of Congress, 1906), 768-78.

17. 24 May 1783, *The Works of John Adams...*, ed. Charles Francis Adams, 10 vols. (1850-56; reprint ed. Freeport, N.Y.: Books for Libraries Press, 1969), 8:60.

18. See, for example, John Adams to James Sullivan, 16 August 1785; to John Hancock, 2 September 1785, Adams Papers microfilm, reel 111.

19. Peterson, "Thomas Jefferson and Commercial Policy," p. 590.

20. Irving Brant, *James Madison*, vol. 3, *Father of the Constitution, 1787-1800* (Indianapolis: Bobbs-Merrill, 1950), pp. 245-54.

21. For a lucid exposition of the antithesis that Americans and English Opposition writers perceived between commerce and virtue, see J. G. A. Pocock, "Virtue and Commerce in the Eighteenth Century," *Journal of Interdisciplinary History* 1 (1972): 119-34.

22. Adams to Benjamin Rush, 28 December 1807, in Biddle, *Old Family Letters*, 1:176.

23. Quoted in Gordon Wood, *The Creation of the American Republic, 1776-1787* (Chapel Hill: Univ. of North Carolina Press, 1969), p. 94.

24. *Warren-Adams Letters*, 2 vols. (1917-25; reprint ed., New York: AMS Press, 1972), 1: 22-23.

25. Ibid., 2: 187.

26. Adams Papers microfilm, reel 111.

27. To John Adams, 21 July 1785, ibid., reel 365.

28. To Simeon Deane, 16 May 1781, *The Dean Papers, 1779-1781,* New York Historical Society, *Collections . . . for the Year 1889* (Boston, 1890), p. 341, also p. 336.

29. Gilbert, *To the Farewell Address,* pp. 60-63, 66; Gabriel Bonnot, abbe de Mably, *Remarks Concerning the Government and the Laws of the United States of America . . .* (Dublin: Moncrieffe, 1785), pp. 173-85; Gabriel Riquetti, comte de Mirabeau, *Considerations on the Order of Cincinnatus* (London: J. Johnson, 1785), pp. 214ff.; Guillaume Thomas Francois Raynal, "An Address to the Independent Citizens of America," *Lloyd's Evening Post,* 22-23 December 1785. My attention was drawn to the views of these writers on the relationship of commerce and republicanism by an excellent, unpublished paper by Gerald J. Ghelfi, "European Opinions of American Republicanism During the 'Critical Period.' 1781-1789."

30. Mably, *Remarks,* pp. 184-85.

31. According to Silas Deane in letter to John Jay, 8 April 1781, *Deane Papers,* p. 299.

32. *Notes on the State of Virginia,* in Koch and Peden, *Thomas Jefferson,* p. 285; to Elbridge Gerry, 13 May 1797, ibid., p. 543.

33. Quoted in Wood, *Creation of the American Republic,* p. 113.

34. To John Jay, 6 December 1785, Adams Papers microfilm, reel 111.

35. Elbridge Gerry Papers, Manuscript Division.

36. Report on Letters From the American Ministers in Europe, 20 December 1783, in *The Papers of Thomas Jefferson,* ed. Julian P. Boyd et al. (Princeton: Princeton Univ. Press, 1950-), 6:397.

37. To Charles Van Hogendorp, 13 October 1785, in Koch and Peden, *Thomas Jefferson,* p. 384.

38. To John Jay, 6 December 1785, Adams Papers microfilm, reel 111.

39. Diary, 11 November 1782, *Diary and Autobiography of John Adams,* ed. Lyman Butterfield et al., 4 vols. (Cambridge: Harvard Univ. Press, 1961), 3:51.

40. Wood, *Creation of the American Republic,* pp. 30-32. See also Bailyn, *Ideological Origins,* pp. 46-48, 78.

41. Gilbert, *To the Farewell Address,* p. 17.

42. Bailyn, *Ideological Origins,* p. 55ff. See also Wood, *Creation of the American Republic,* p. 34ff.

43. In Edwin G. Burrows and Michael Wallace, "The American Revolution: The Ideology and Psychology of National Liberation," *Perspectives in American History* 6 (1972): 221, 297n.

44. To Benjamin Rush, 23 May 1807, in Schutz and Adair, *Spur of Fame,* p. 89.

45. Andrew Burnaby, *Travels Through the Middle Settlements in North America in the Years 1759 and 1760* . . . (New York: A. Wessels, 1904), p. 149.

46. To Lord Kames, 11 April 1767, *The Writings of Benjamin Franklin*, ed. Albert H. Smyth, 10 vols. (New York: Macmillan, 1905-07), 5:21.

47. To Nathan Webb, 12 October 1755, in Schutz and Adair, *Spur of Fame*, p. 81.

48. In Smyth, *Writings of Franklin*, 3:71.

49. To Lord Kames, 3 January 1760, ibid., 4:4.

50. John Dickinson, *The Late Regulations Respecting the British Colonies*, in Bernard Bailyn, ed., *Pamphlets of the American Revolution*, vol. 1, *1750-1765* (Cambridge: Belknap Press of Harvard Univ. Press, 1965), p. 687.

51. Quoted by Adams, Diary, *Diary and Autobiography*, 2:214.

52. In Boyd, *Papers of Thomas Jefferson*, 1:219.

53. To Silas Deane, in Edmund C. Burnett, ed., *Letters of Members of the Continental Congress*, vol. 1 (Washington: Carnegie Institution, 1921), p. 376.

54. Adams, *Works*, 7: 100.

55. To Silas Deane, 20 December 1776, transcript in editorial office of *Letters of Delegates to Congress*.

56. To Silas Deane, 3 March 1776, in Burnett, *Letters*, 1: 376.

57. To van der Capellen, 21 January 1781, Adams, *Works*, 7: 357; to Edmond Genêt, 9 May 1780, ibid., p. 161.

58. To Samuel Huntington, 25 September 1780, in Francis Wharton, ed., *The Revolutionary Diplomatic Correspondence of the United States*, 6 vols. (Washington: Government Printing Office, 1889), 4: 67-69; to Edmund Jenings, 27 April 1781, Adams papers microfilm, reel 354.

59. To Jean de Neufville, 24 March 1781, ibid., reel 102.

60. To Robert Livingston, 23 June 1783, in Wharton, *Revolutionary Diplomatic Correspondence*, 6: 500; to Edmund Jenings, 18 July 1780, Adams Papers microfilm, reel 352; to the president of Congress, 8 December 1778, ibid., reel 93.

61. Burnett, *Letters*, 1:3.

62. Hutson, *A Decent Respect*, p. 108.

63. John Wendell to Franklin, 30 October 1777, quoted in Stinchcombe, *American Revolution and French Alliance*, p. 11.

64. Adams Papers microfilm, reel 93.

65. Quoted in Gilbert, *To the Farewell Address*, p. 106.

66. Ibid., pp. 89, 96.

67. To John Wendell, transcript in editorial office of *Letters to Delegates to Congress*.

68. *Warren-Adams Letters*, 2: 192.

69. *Diary and Autobiography*, 2: 235.

70. To Samuel Huntington, 17 June 1780, Adams Papers microfilm, reel 100. See also Boyd, *Papers of Thomas Jefferson*, 1: 325; and Richard Henry Lee to Samuel Adams, 29 July 1776; William Whipple to Joseph Whipple, 29 July 1776; and Robert Morris to Horatio Gates, 27 October 1776, transcripts in editorial office of *Letters of Delegates to Congress*.

71. John Adams to Samuel Adams, 28 July 1778, Adams Papers microfilm, reel 93; to Edmund Jenings, 26 April 1780, ibid., reel 351; to Congress, 4 August 1779, Adams, *Works*, 7: 107; and to Genêt, 17 May 1780, ibid., p. 173.

72. So, at least, he is represented by Stourzh, *Hamilton and Republican Government*, pp. 135-39.

73. See, for example, *The Occasional Writer, no. 2* and *Letters on the Study and Use of History* in *Works of the Late Rt. Hon. Henry St. John, Lord Viscount Bolingbroke* (Dublin, 1753), pp. 158, 358, 372, 423, 434. Also Edward Gulick, *Europe's Classical Balance of Power* (Ithaca: Cornell Univ. Press for the American Historical Association, 1955), p. 28.

74. Gilbert, *To the Farewell Address*, p. 22.

75. Autobiography, *Diary and Autobiography*, 4: 38-39.

76. To Mercy Warren, 20 July 1807, in *Collections of the Massachusetts Historical Society*, Ser. 5, 4 (1878): 350.

77. To Landon Carter, 14 April 1776, transcript in editorial office of *Letters of Delegates to Congress*.

78. Adams, Diary, *Diary and Autobiography*, 3: 122.

79. Transcript in editorial office of *Letters of Delegates to Congress*.

80. To Samuel Chase, Adams Papers microfilm, reel 89; to Jay, Adams, *Works*, 7: 610.

81. Quoted in Stourzh, *Hamilton and Republican Government*, p. 153.

82. Ibid., p. 255, n. 89.

83. Quoted in Stinchcombe, *American Revolution and French Alliance,* pp. 25-26. For John Adams's agreement on this point, see his letter to Izard, 25 September 1778, Adams Papers microfilm, reel 93; to Jenings, 11 June 1780, ibid., reel 352; to Franklin, 16 April and 24 May 1782, ibid., reel 107.

84. *Notes on the State of Virginia*, in Koch and Peden, *Thomas Jefferson*, p. 285.

85. To Jay, 19 July 1785, Adams Papers microfilm, reel 111; to R. H. Lee, 24 December 1785, ibid., reel 111; to Jay, 27 October 1786, ibid., reel 112.

86. To Samuel Huntington, 16 June 1780, ibid., reel 100. See also his letter to John Heath, 10 July 1778, ibid., reel 93; and to C. W. F. Dumas,

19 May 1781, ibid., reel 102; also Adams, Diary, *Diary and Autobiography*, 3: 61, 68.

87. Adams to Edmund Jenings, 25 April 1780, Adams Papers microfilm, reel 351; to R. H. Lee, 24 December 1785, ibid., reel 112.

88. To Jenings, 18 July 1780, ibid., reel 352.

89. To Robert Livingston, 5 February 1783, in Wharton, *Revolutionary Diplomatic Correspondence*, 6: 243. See also Adams, Diary, *Diary and Autobiography*, 3: 105, 115-16; Adams to Jenings, 18 April 1783, Adams Papers microfilm, reel 108; to Matthew Robinson, 13 December 1786, ibid., reel 113.

90. Rush to Adams, 14 August 1805, in Adair and Schutz, *Spur of Fame*, p. 32; also 21 September 1805, ibid., p. 36.

91. Adams, Autobiography, *Diary and Autobiography*, 3: 337.

92. To Benjamin Rush, 19 December 1808, in Biddle, *Old Family Letters*, p. 205. See also *Boston Patriot*, 18 July 1809.

93. To Monroe, 11 July 1790, in Boyd, *Papers of Thomas Jefferson*, 17: 25; to Jay, 23 August 1785, ibid., 8: 427.

94. Fifth Annual Address to Congress, 3 December 1793, in *The Writings of George Washington*, ed. John C. Fitzpatrick, 39 vols. (Washington: Government Printing Office, 1931-44), 33: 166; First Annual Address to Congress, 8 January 1790, ibid., 30: 491.

95. *Plain Truth*, in *The Papers of Benjamin Franklin*, ed. Leonard W. Labaree et al. (New Haven: Yale University Press, 1959-), 3: 203.

96. To Robert Livingston, 19 July 1783, *The Correspondence and Public Papers of John Jay*, ed. Henry P. Johnston, vol. 3 (1890-93; reprint ed., New York: B. Franklin, 1970), p. 55.

97. Quoted by Silas Deane, Diary, 3 October 1774, transcript in editorial office of *Letters of Delegates to Congress*.

98. Speech at Virginia Ratifying Convention, 10 June 1788, *The Papers of John Marshall*, ed. Herbert A. Johnson, vol. 1 (Chapel Hill: Univ. of North Carolina Press in association with the Institute of Early American History and Culture, 1974), p. 262.

99. Quoted by John Adams, Notes of Debates in Congress, 26-27 September 1774, Diary, *Diary and Autobiography*, 2: 139.

100. To Patrick Henry, 14 February 1785, in *The Letters of Richard Henry Lee*, ed. James C. Ballagh, vol. 2 (1911-14; reprint ed., New York: Da Capo, 1970), p. 334.

101. 8 August 1785, Adams Papers microfilm, reel 111.

102. For a similar view, see Lawrence S. Kaplan, *Colonies Into Nation: American Diplomacy, 1763-1801* (New York: Macmillan, 1974), pp. 189-91.

103. Gilbert, *To the Farewell Address*, p. 143; Morgenthau, *In Defense of the National Interest*, pp. 4-33.

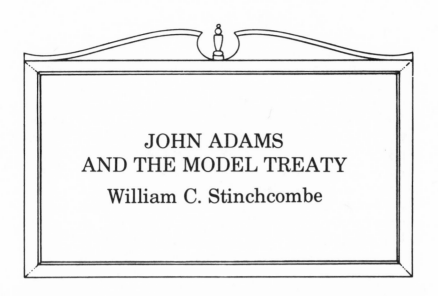

# JOHN ADAMS
# AND THE MODEL TREATY
## William C. Stinchcombe

In the eyes of their supporters, the Declaration of
Independence, the Model Treaty, and the Articles of
Confederation were interlocking. The documents supported each other, and each was indispensable to the
establishment of independent government in 1776.
Members of Congress saw a direct line between the
Declaration of Independence and the Model Treaty.
Richard Henry Lee noted in his motion for independence
"that it is expedient forthwith to take the most effectual
measures for forming foreign Alliances."[1] John Adams
agreed with his colleague's reasoning, observing that
"Confederation will be necessary for our internal concord, and alliance may be so for our external defense."[2]
The Model Treaty was the linchpin of the drive for foreign
recognition. It indicated the limited, almost entirely
commercial, relations that members of Congress sought
with European powers.

John Adams has been recognized by historians as "the
chief architect of the Model Treaty and its accompanying
instructions." Adams's work has been credited with
setting forth America's posture toward Europe in the
early years of the republic. The reasoning and the
definitions of diplomacy contained in the Model Treaty
were, according to one scholar, "entirely alien to the spirit

of the diplomatic practice of the time."[3] Such a view exaggerates both the importance of the Model Treaty and John Adams's contribution to revolutionary diplomacy. Adams's conception of strictly commercial diplomacy was not new but adapted from diplomatic ideas and practices current in Europe. The previous century had witnessed numerous attempts to separate the political and commercial facets of diplomacy, efforts advanced by the Protestant merchant classes in the Netherlands and Great Britain. Adams, furthermore, served only on an *ad hoc* committee to draft the Model Treaty, not on the Committee of Secret Correspondence, which appointed diplomats and furnished their instructions.

We can see a marked difference between Adams's ideology in composing the treaty and the Committee's conduct of foreign policy from 1776 to 1778. Viewed from the Committee's perspective, the Model Treaty was just that—a model, a statement of aspiration for the future. But Adams's statement did not depart from the wishes of many members of Congress. Inadequate as a formula for short-term policy, the Model Treaty can best be considered as a plan for postwar commitments to Europe.

The Model Treaty reflected the widespread belief that American foreign policy should allow only commercial connections with Europe. The treaty's provisions emphasized the value of the most-favored-nation clause, of open rather than closed commercial systems. Political alliances were to be shunned, and the United States would instead rely on the liberating effects of commerce to avoid struggles within the European balance of power. The Model Treaty did not authorize United States representatives to offer an alliance to France if it recognized the United States. In the instructions accompanying the Model Treaty, Congress went only so far as to promise France that the United States would not side with Great Britain in the event of a war between Great Britain and France.

Congress passed the Model Treaty by a unanimous vote, but within less than two years it unanimously approved an alliance with France, the provisions of which directly contradicted many tenets of the Model Treaty. In both cases the unanimity of Congress doubtless reflected a desire to demonstrate unity to the outside world. When it approved the French alliance in 1778, Congress was meeting in York, Pennsylvania, as the British occupied Philadelphia, New York, and Newport. Foremost among the issues facing Congress in 1778 were the devastating effects of British sea power on American commerce and military strategy. Members of Congress had to consider the difficulties of sustaining an army, not to mention a credit and currency policy reduced to shambles. Reflections on the proper sort of foreign policy received little attention. The paramount need in 1778 was for foreign aid in any form.

The unanimous vote for the Model Treaty had not indicated what an important segment, if not a majority, of Congressmen thought necessary to entice France to aid or recognize the United States. At the time of its passage the Model Treaty answered no short-term questions about the foreign policy required to achieve independence. The document had a commercial premise, offering promised American commerce only after the achievement of independence. Neither the correspondence of the time nor the Journals of Congress include any extended debate or action on specific questions concerning a future alliance, questions such as access to the fisheries, navigation rights on the Mississippi River, or the probable difficulties of justifying cooperation with a Catholic monarch. The Model Treaty as approved in 1776 did not require members of Congress to compromise strongly-defended sectional interests. The treaty expressed ideals, and the dominant mood at its passage was seen in one Congressman's statement that "foreign agencies, I hope, will fill our ports with ships from all parts of the world." The reservations suggested by another member who feared

71

that "people are too sanguine relative to Commerce" were held in abeyance in the summer and fall of 1776.[4]

The change of policy between the Model Treaty of 1776 and the French alliance of 1778 can be better understood if we examine the conduct of foreign policy by the Committee of Secret Correspondence. At various times the Committee's membership included Richard Henry Lee, Robert Morris, Silas Deane, Benjamin Franklin, and others such as John Witherspoon and William Hooper. Committee members did not openly disagree with the Model Treaty, which had been drawn up by another committee. Rather, they ignored it as they sought to secure much-needed supplies from Europe. The Committee regarded commerce as the best, if not the only, asset in securing French and Spanish aid. Robert Morris stated the Committee's position clearly: "If the court of France open their eyes to their own interest, and think the commerce of North America will compensate for the expense and evil of a war with Great Britain, they may readily create a diversion, and afford us succors that will change the fate of affairs." Morris added, "I dare assert that whatever European power possesses the pre-emption of it [commerce] must of consequence become the richest and most potent in Europe." And "I am sure if they lost this golden opportunity they will never have another."[5]

The Committee concentrated on supplying American needs, allowing a certain self-interest to some merchants among its members. Two weeks after the Model Treaty's passage the Committee gave its agent in France, Silas Deane, additional instructions.[6] The Model Treaty went unmentioned except for a note that more information would follow when Benjamin Franklin, the newly elected commissioner, left for France. The Committee directed Deane to try to persuade the French Court to send twenty ships of line to make a surprise attack on Lord Howe at New York. The tenor of the dispatch can be seen in its one statement on future policy: "If France means to befriend us, or wishes us well, they should send us the succors in good muskets, blankets, cloths, coatings, and proper stuff for tents, also in ammunition; but not like the Venetians, wait until we are beat, and then send assistance."[7]

The Committee's only explicit instructions on alliances are of interest in seeing how far these directions diverged from the Model Treaty's premises. At the end of December 1776, when New York had fallen and the British threatened to take Philadelphia, the Committee sought help from France and Spain. The hesitancy that some members of Congress felt about political connections with these powers was now forgotten. The Committee instructed the American commissioners in France to present an offer of political treaties based on territorial exchanges and traditional considerations under the balance of power. An alliance, especially a military one, was desired. For Spain, the Committee agreed to declare war on Portugal if the Spanish Court would cede to the United States navigation rights on the Mississippi.[8] Other American diplomats received instructions to make no agreements that would hinder the proposed arrangements with France and Spain.

Congress concerned itself with preparing for the British offensive of 1777, spending little time on foreign policy as such. Scattered but growing protests decried the French delay in entering the war, but most members of Congress felt satisfied with the renewed assurances of greatly increased aid and supplies. Richard Henry Lee went beyond this position when he wrote his brother Arthur in Paris:

> In my judgement, and it is an opinion founded on the most accurate information, the Independence, and security of N[orth] America cannot be said to be certain until an Alliance with Spain & France is procured, and in consequence, the British Arms and Arts not solely employed for our ruin. You may be assured *that* this is of infinite consequence to your Country and therefore you conduct yourself accordingly.[9]

After the American victory at Saratoga, the French Court offered the United States an alliance—an alliance based on a commercial treaty following the Model Treaty and a defensive treaty in which France and the United States would be bound by mutual guarantees. Both nations were to pledge no separate peace with England, and the United States to promise to guarantee French West Indian possessions. The American commissioners in Paris, Deane, Franklin, and Lee, disregarded their original instructions from Congress and quickly concluded the alliance in February 1778.[10] The Congressional reaction to the news of the alliance supported the commissioners' departure from their instructions. After less than half a day's debate, Congress approved the commercial and defensive treaties with France.[11] There was no outspoken criticism of the defensive treaty, which was soon published in all newspapers; those who had reservations mentioned them only to close associates or relatives.[12]

The reactions of Congress revealed once more that the necessities of independence would override previous attitudes on policy. Long-term goals such as the Model Treaty had been deferred. But even at the time Congress ratified the defensive alliance with France many Americans still considered commerce the one solid base upon which to make foreign connections. The images used by William Livingston when he heard of the peace proposals by Great Britain in 1778 and the alliance with France are suggestive. "France and Great Britain seem to be like two great merchants recurring to America for a market and I hope we shall not be such block-heads as to sell our commodities too cheap."[13]

John Adams continued to serve in Congress as the Model Treaty's prescriptions went unheeded. His reaction before leaving for France in 1778 can be characterized as one of studied ambiguity. Before the passage of the Declaration of Independence Adams had declared in a letter to a Massachusetts friend that he wanted "no political connection, or military assistance, or indeed naval from France. I wish for nothing but commerce, a mere marine treaty with them."[14] This was to be his most extreme statement, for after independence he noted that "Had a Declaration of Independence been made seven Months ago it would have been attended with many great and glorious effects. . . . We might before this Hour, have formed Alliances with foreign states."[15]

In considering alliances, Adams showed consistency only in his interpretation of French motives and policy. French self-interest and only self-interest would lead France to aid the United States, he believed. Any inducements that the Americans might make would be of little significance. Correct in his judgment of the French, Adams did not attempt to defend or apply the thoughts expressed in the Model Treaty. Probably he himself had little commitment to applying it if such a policy would risk deferring independence or prolonging the war. Indeed, Adams did not refer to the Model Treaty during the war and returned to it only when writing his autobiography more than twenty-five years later. In this retrospective view he stressed the Model Treaty's importance.[16]

Among historians emphasizing the Model Treaty the most notable is Felix Gilbert, who has argued that the Model Treaty had important influence on early American diplomacy. Gilbert contends that the American view of the world and foreign policy evolved from beliefs developed by the English radical Whig opposition. The numerous wars of the eighteenth century saw the appearance of a small but consistent public opposition to Great Britain's involvement in Continental alliances. These alliances, the critics charged. stemmed from the king's dual role in Great Britain and the Duchy of Hanover. Because of the alliances needed to maintain Hanover and British influence in Europe, lucrative colonial commerce was lost. Spokesmen of a nascent isolationist philosophy, the radical Whigs advanced a position in which commerce and colonial possessions were considered more important than involvements in the European balance of power and alliances.

In the popular mind the foremost advocate of this new direction in foreign policy was William Pitt the elder during the last years of the Seven Years' War. The tradition of open debate and a limited freedom of the press allowed issues concerning foreign policy and national interest to be explored and then exported to the American colonies. There they were quickly accepted and adapted to American conditions.[17] Gilbert's thesis on foreign policy is thus similar to Bernard Bailyn's on the acceptance of Enlightenment ideas in eighteenth-century America.[18]

Gilbert, however, continues his argument beyond Bailyn's position by linking American ideas in foreign policy with the Continental philosophes. The philosophes' ideas on diplomacy concentrated on the evils of secret diplomacy as practiced by monarchs. A period of constant warfare led them to conclude that the balance of power caused, not prevented, war. A growing number of philosophes also attacked stringent mercantilist policies, particularly chartered monopolies in trade with some colonies. In a period of rapidly increasing trade, thinkers were reconsidering the effects of commerce on society.

We cannot precisely determine the philosophes' influence on the independence movement in the United States. The philosophes discussed by Gilbert went virtually unmentioned in the American debates and correspondence of the time. Part of the difficulty is, as Gilbert says, that "most of the eighteenth-century philosophes were French."[19] The long-time rivalry between Great Britain and France, French governmental absolutism and Catholicism, and the limited commercial and educational ties between the American colonies and France all made that country an unlikely source for American interpretations of commerce and foreign relations.

Nevertheless, the influence of European thought and experience cannot be discounted, particularly in John Adams's case. Adams is said by Gilbert to have taken the idea of the separation of commercial and political treaties from the Treaty of Utrecht between Great Britain and France.[20] Not until the peace negotiations of 1782, however, did Adams mention the Treaty of Utrecht.[21] Nonetheless, it is true that most treaties in the eighteenth century offered variations of the Treaties of Utrecht, in which the French and English agreed to a political truce prior to final agreement on the commercial treaty.[22] The separation of commercial and political treaties was common to Dutch diplomacy and often to Dutch-English treaties in the seventeenth century, and Adams was conscious of this heritage.

Other provisions of the Model Treaty had also appeared in treaties before the Treaty of Utrecht. In 1674 and again in 1688 the English recognized the Dutch objective of "free ships make free goods." In a commercial treaty with Sweden in 1681 the Dutch won the most-favored-nation principle, and in following decades they sought to extend it to other nations.[23] By the end of the seventeenth century, a growing belief, centered in the province of Holland, held that alliances should be avoided and that the maintenance of commerce should be the goal of the States General. According to one scholar, by 1720 the Dutch sought "to avoid entanglement in alliances, even in those which were purely defensive."[24] Adams may well have considered examples from Dutch and English history when formulating the Model Treaty in 1776.

The commercial ideals identified with the Model Treaty and Americans were less distinctive than usually recognized. Americans of 1776 fit the general pattern of a Protestant, merchant, capitalist class trying to achieve commercial stability during the eighteenth century's wars. The bonds of religion and politics between the Netherlands and England had been close in the seventeenth and the first half of the eighteenth century. In their foreign policy the Dutch had experienced the disputes and debated the ideas commonly attributed to the radical Whigs and philosophes, and the Dutch did so in a much earlier period. The Dutch, moreover, had many attributes that bore at least a superficial resemblance to those of Americans in 1776. The Netherlands was a republic of sorts, in which the nobility had little influence. The merchants and the church made a highly literate group within the society; debates concerning national interest and foreign policy were carried on in books, pamphlets, and the States General. Dutch merchants increasingly supported a policy of neutrality, whereby military commitments would be limited and commercial rights preserved in wartime. An intense debate continued throughout the Netherlands, punctuated by frequent clashes of the Stadholder's territorial ambitions and the merchants' desire for neutrality and the preservation of commerce.[25]

A broad similarity existed between merchant classes in Great Britain, the United States, and the Netherlands. Mainly Protestant, the merchants lived in societies that had developed a working toleration of other religions. Their outlook was international. They were republican or perhaps anti-statist in opposing the government's power to determine exclusive commercial rights as exemplified by the East Indies Company in Great Britain and the Netherlands. They supported open debate on foreign policy and religion, and except in Great Britain, they had positions of status and influence within their societies.

The Dutch experience was known to one Continental philosophe who had considerable influence on John Adams and members of Congress, the Baron de Montesquieu.[26] Montesquieu's *De l'Esprit des Lois* was widely read and quoted in the American struggle against Great Britain. Americans who cited Montesquieu stressed first his conception of liberty and second his ideas on commerce. Montesquieu had argued that only republics were suited for commerce, repeatedly citing the Netherlands as a prime example. He acknowledged that Great Britain had preserved freedom of religion, commerce, and liberty, but he was puzzled why this was so.[27] During the

American Revolution it was noted that one of the French officers visiting Philadelphia was "the grandson to President Montesquieu, whose name is so dear to every lover of liberty and humanity."[28]

John Adams not only read Montesquieu, but quoted him frequently.[29] Adams also knew the Dutch example, and in the first years of the Revolution he began an extensive reading program in Dutch history, in which he detected many parallels of interest to Americans. To make sure that the ten-year-old John Quincy Adams would not miss the importance of "the History of the Causes which have produced the late Revolution of our Government," he sent him a lengthy reading list in European history. Adams focused on the Dutch as one of the more instructive examples.

> But above all others, I would recommend to your study, the History of the Flemish Confederacy, by which the seven united Provinces of the Netherlands, emancipated themselves from the Domination of Spain.
> There are several good Histories of this great Revolution. Sir William Temple is short but elegant, and entertaining. Another Account of this Period was written by Puffendorf, and another by Grotius.[30]

Adams considered freedom of commerce inseparable from other liberties Americans wanted to secure. A free commerce he placed in the same category as other freedoms achieved in Great Britain and the Netherlands, namely, the right of self-government, freedom of localities, and freedom of religion. Other eighteenth-century thinkers had also emphasized the importance of commerce. The writer Jacques de Serionne argued that commerce must be the basis of alliances between nations.[31] Another spokesman for freedom of commerce, Jean Melon, likened the battle for a free commerce to the earlier struggle for religious liberty. Melon went so far as to argue that only a republican government could provide the societal basis for widespread commerce.[32] Thus Adams's premises in the Model Treaty were familiar rather than new, the ideas available to him in European history and writings. Adams referred to these ideas often, always assuming that the society he cherished would uphold religious freedom and toleration, limited government, and free commerce.[33]

In 1780 Adams was appointed United States minister to the Netherlands. Not his diplomacy but his reaction to Dutch society should be noted. By the time he reached the Netherlands Adams had observed Spanish and French society, seeing them through a prism of Protestant commercial values. In Spain he saw "nothing but Signs of Poverty and Misery," the people "ragged and dirty, and the Houses universally nothing but Mire, Smoke, Fleas, and Lice." Nowhere did he find symptoms of "Commerce or even of internal Traffic, no Appearance of Manufactures or Industry." Later in France Adams complained, "Luxury, dissipation, and Effeminacy, are pretty nearly at the same degree of Excess here, and in every part of Europe."[34]

But when Adams had an opportunity to reflect on the Netherlands, he found a society compatible with his preconceived views. He was pleased with Holland, a country like no other in Europe due to the "Effect of Industry, and the Work of Art. The Frugality, Industry, Cleanliness &c here, deserve the imitation of My Countrymen."[35] Later he described the country as "a Protestant, a Republican and a Commercial Nation," the people "Protestant, Calvinist, Antiepiscopalians, Tolerant, Republican, Commercial."[36] That the Puritan or Protestant ethic had reality for Adams is clear from his reactions. Admiring the Dutch, he nevertheless cautioned against emulating their commercial habits, because this would lead a person to seek only profit and eschew the larger issues of life.[37]

In 1781 Adams submitted a memorial to the States General advocating Dutch recognition of the United States. Although he envisioned close commercial ties between the two countries, commerce was not the primary reason for recognition. He mentioned the early Dutch settlers in New York and New Jersey, the compatibility of religion between the two countries, and the common form of government. Moreover, the Netherlands displayed a "liberality of sentiments in those momentous points of freedom of inquiry, the right of private judgement, and liberty of conscience."[38] Then Adams mentioned commerce. John Adams saw in the Netherlands a society similar to the new one he was trying to create, and he hoped for Dutch support on that basis, not only because of balance-of-power or commercial considerations.

For Adams the Model Treaty expressed principles culled from the history of Dutch and English government and society in the previous century. Commerce had a firm position in Adams's constellation of ideals, but it remained inseparable from morality and virtue, republicanism and self-government. The Model Treaty reflected Adams's moral view of the world, his moral interpretation of commerce and diplomacy. Adams's colleagues on the Committee of Secret Correspondence directed American foreign policy according to the older, more familiar, standards of European diplomacy. The Model Treaty revealed more about John Adams's cast of mind than it did about the actual practice of the Continental Congress in diplomacy. Nevertheless, Adams's ideas also had wide acceptance, and commerce did become a pillar of future diplomacy. Seeking autonomy from European wars and protection for their commerce, Americans used the Model Treaty as the basis for a number of treaties negotiated with European powers after independence. But it was not the dawning of a new age in diplomacy. American diplomacy proceeded along the lines indicated by the Protestant merchant classes in the previous century.

# NOTES

1. 7 June 1776, Worthington C. Ford, ed., *Journals of the Continental Congress* (Washington: Government Printing Office, 1904-1937), V, 425.

2. John Adams to Abigail Adams, 17 May 1776, Lyman H. Butterfield, ed., *Adams Family Correspondence* (New York: Atheneum, 1965), I, 410-12.

3. Felix Gilbert, *The Beginnings of American Foreign Policy* (New York: Harper Torchbooks, 1965), pp. 49, 54.

4. For the debate on the Model Treaty, see Ford, ed., *Journals of C.C.*, V, 18, 20 July, 22, 27, 29 Aug., 17, 24, 26 Sept. 1776, 575-89, 594, 696, 709-10, 718, 768-79, 813-17, 827-28; quotes from William Whipple to to John Langdon, 18 May 1776; John Penn to [Thomas Person], 28 June 1776, Edmund C. Burnett, ed., *Letters of Members of Continental Congress* (Washington: Carnegie Institution of Washington, 1921-1936), I, 456, 514.

5. Robert Morris to Commissioners in Paris, 21 Dec. 1776, Francis Wharton, ed., *Diplomatic Correspondence of American Revolution* (Washington: Government Printing Office, 1889), I, 235-36.

6. Committee of Secret Correspondence to Silas Deane, 1 Oct. 1776, ibid., 157-61.

7. Ibid.

8. Committee of Secret Correspondence to Commisioners in Paris, 30 Dec. 1776, ibid., 240-41.

9. Richard Henry Lee to Arthur Lee, 20 Apr. 1777, James C. Ballagh, ed., *The Letters of Richard Henry Lee* (New York: Macmillan, 1911), I, 277-82; for Adams, see John Adams to James Warren, 3 May 1777, Burnett, ed., *LMCC*, II, 334-35.

10. Franklin & Deane to President of Congress, 8 Feb. 1778, Wharton, ed., *Dip. Corr.*, I, 491-92.

11. 2, 4 May 1778, Ford, ed., *Journals of C.C.*, XI, 417-57.

12. William Stinchcombe, *The American Revolution and the French Alliance* (Syracuse: Syracuse Univ. Press, 1969), 16, 20.

13. William Livingston to Henry Laurens, 7 May 1778, Henry Laurens Papers, South Carolina Historical Society.

14. John Adams to John Winthrop, 23 June 1776, Burnett, ed., *LMCC*, I, 502.

15. John Adams to Abigail Adams, 2 July 1776, Butterfield, ed., *Adams Fam. Corr.*, II, 29. The suspension points are in the original.

16. Lyman H. Butterfield, ed., *Diary and Autobiography of John Adams* (New York: Atheneum, 1965), III, 337-38.

17. Gilbert, *The Beginnings,* pp. 22-43.

18. Bernard Bailyn, "Political Experience and Enlightenment

Ideas in Eighteenth-Century America," *American Historical Review*, LXVII(Jan. 1962), 344.

19. Gilbert, *The Beginnings*, quote, p. 58; also pp. 57-66.

20. Ibid., pp. 50-51; Samuel F. Bemis, *The Diplomacy of the American Revolution* (New York: Appleton-Century Co., 1935), p. 46; Gerald Stourzh, *Benjamin Franklin and American Foreign Policy* (Chicago: University of Chicago Press, 1969), 2nd ed., pp. 124-25. Stourzh, following Gilbert, suggests that Adams might have used the treaty between James II and Louis XIV of 1686, declaring the neutrality of the American colonies, but the separation of political and commercial treaties, not the concept of neutrality, is important here.

21. 25, 29 Nov. 1782, Butterfield, ed., *Diary & Autobiography of Adams*, III, 73-76, 79-81.

22. Jacob M. Price, *France and the Chesapeake* (Ann Arbor: Univ. of Michigan Press, 1973), I, 524-25, 530.

23. Alice Carter, *Neutrality or Commitment: The Evolution of Dutch Foreign Policy, 1667-1795* (London: Edward Arnold, 1975), pp. 15-17, 37.

24. Ibid., p. 50.

25. Ibid., pp. 85, 95; J. W. Smit, "The Netherlands and Europe in the Seventeenth and Eighteenth Centuries," J. S. Bromley and E. H. Kossmann, eds., *Britain and the Netherlands in Europe and Asia* (London: Macmillan, 1968), pp. 14, 15, 16, 23, 26; J. Roorda, "The Ruling Classes in Holland in the Seventeenth Century," J. S. Bromley & E. H. Kossmann, eds., *Britain and the Netherlands* (Groningen: J. B. Wolters, 1964), II, 117, 124, 132; H. Wansink, "Holland and Six Allies: the Republic of the Seven United Provinces," J. S. Bromley and E. H. Kossmann, eds., *Britain and the Netherlands* (The Hague: Martinus Nijhoff, 1971), IV, 142; Charles Wilson, *Profit and Power* (London: Macmillan, 1957), p. 17; Alice Carter, *Getting, Spending, and Investing in Early Modern Times* (Assen: Van Gorcum, 1975), pp. 76-106, 142-73.

26. Paul M. Spurlin, *Montesquieu in America, 1760-1801* (Baton Rouge: Louisiana State Univ. Press, 1940), pp. 154-57; Bailyn, "Political Experience and the Enlightenment," 344.

27. Charles L. le Baron de Montesquieu, *L'Esprit des Lois* (Berlin: A. Asher, n.d.) rev. ed., pp. 297-99, 301-02.

28. *Annapolis Gazette,* 29 Dec. 1780.

29. Summer 1759, 26 June, 3 July 1760, Apr. 1778, Butterfield, ed., *Diary & Autobiography of Adams*, I, 115-18, 123, 142, 143; IV, 67; Adams stated that he had to read Montesquieu and others who were "good civil Writers." Jan. 1759, ibid., I, 73; Spurlin, *Montesquieu in America*, pp. 119-20.

30. John Adams to John Q. Adams, 27 July 1777; John Adams to

Abigail Adams, 21 July 1777, Butterfield, ed., *Adams Fam. Corr.,* II, 289-90; 286-87.

31. Jacques Accarias de Serionne, *Le Commerce de la Hollande* (Amsterdam: Francois Changuion, 1768), I, 38, 39.

32. Jean F. Melon, *Essay Politique sur le Commerce* (Amsterdam: Francois Changuion, 1754), 2nd ed., 59, 139; also see Francois de Forbannois, *Elémens du Commerce* (Amsterdam: Francois Changuion, 1755), 2nd ed.; — Eobald, *La Liberté de la Navigation et du Commerce* (Amsterdam: 1780); Jacques Accarias de Serionne, *La Richesse de la Hollande* (London: Aux Depens de la Compagnie, 1778), 2 vols.; Jean LeClerc, *Histoire des Provinces Unies,* (Amsterdam: Z. Chatelain, 1728), II.

33. J. G. A. Pocock, "Virtue and Commerce in the Eighteenth Century," *Journal of Interdisciplinary History,* 3 (Summer 1972), 119-34; H. Trevor Colbourn, *The Lamp of Experience* (New York: W. W. Norton & Co., 1974), pp. 55, 95.

34. 30 Dec. 1779, Butterfield, ed., *Diary & Autobiography of Adams,* II, 419; John Adams to Abigail Adams, 3 June 1778, Butterfield, ed., *Adams Fam. Corr.* (Cambridge: Harvard Univ. Press, 1973), III, 32.

35. John Adams to Abigail Adams, 4 Sept. 1780, ibid., 410.

36. John Adams to Richard Cranch, 17 June, 2 July 1782, ibid., IV, 332, 340.

37. John Adams to Abigail Adams, 18 Dec. 1780, 18 Apr. 1781, ibid., 34-35, 108-10.

38. John Adams to States General, 19 Apr. 1781, Wharton, ed., *Dip. Corr.,* IV, 370-76, quote from 373.

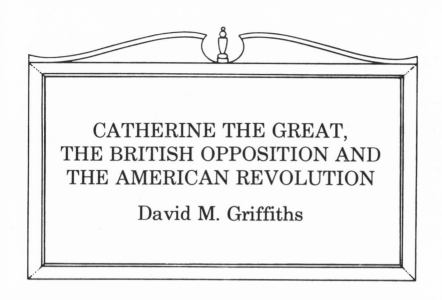

# CATHERINE THE GREAT, THE BRITISH OPPOSITION AND THE AMERICAN REVOLUTION

David M. Griffiths

Prevalent in both Soviet and Western scholarship concerning Catherine the Great and her attitude toward the American Revolution is a cluster of intertwined presuppositions. The American Revolution is commonly portrayed as bearing a message that was at the same time radical, distinct and universally valid. It was radical to the degree that it presented a blatant challenge not simply to British Imperial policy, but to the existing European order in its entirety. It was distinct in the sense that this challenge could be perceived by ruling monarchs and their opposed subjects alike, even if the specific lines of demarcation were not always fully appreciated. And it was universally valid inasmuch as monarchs and subjects were as one in assuming that the American experience was potentially transferable to their own situations. By declaring their independence from Great Britain in principle, and proceeding to enforce it on the field of battle, then, the American revolutionaries are perceived as pursuing something more novel than emancipation from foreign rule; they were engaged in a quest for political and—to a lesser degree—socio-economic democracy. As such, the struggle is commonly described as the introduction to the era of revolution, an identifiable prelude to general rebellion whose leitmotif

85

sounded ominous to the sensitive ears of threatened monarchs throughout Europe.

Given the depth of feeling aroused by the contest and the value-impregnated terms to which it presumably lent currency, it follows inevitably that Catherine II, as one of the chief bulwarks of the ancien régime, could not but feel personally threatened by the events transpiring across the ocean, fearful as she was that her own subjects would imitate the example pioneered by the American revolutionaries.[1] In order to ascertain the extent to which this cluster of presuppositions actually pertains to Catherine II, to her political consciousness and her policy decisions, it will be necessary to probe beyond the ready-made perspectives so prevalent in the existing scholarship to the substance of Catherine's own writings, unofficial as well as official, for clues to her attitude toward the American rebels.

Our suspicions are immediately aroused by a preliminary inspection of the political language employed by the empress, not only within the context of the American Revolution, but that of international relations as a whole; for we find her applying with great frequency precisely those words—"liberty," "independence" and "republic"—so beloved of the rebelling colonists. The most obvious conclusion one may draw is that the empress was not employing the words in the same sense as the Americans. And if this preliminary surmise be true, may Catherine II be expected to fear a rebellion to whose terminology she imparted different meanings? Hence, by extension, would she be likely to abhor a rebellion whose message she failed to fathom? There is something obviously amiss here.

Our initial suspicions are reinforced by an examination of the historical precedents to which she applied this terminology. First of all, the empress tended to equate the American rebellion with that of the Dutch against Spanish domination, a struggle that dragged out for years before eventually culminating in self-determination and then independence for the former Spanish Netherlands. Because of its striking parallels with the War for American Independence, Nikita Panin, director of Russia's foreign affairs since 1763, would grasp at the Spanish-Dutch armistice of 1609 as the logical pattern for his own efforts in 1780 to mediate a solution to Anglo-American hostilities.[2] Still closer at hand was another precedent, one to which the empress herself had recourse: the valiant Corsican struggle to assert independence, first from Genoa, and subsequently from France. Both precedents struck the empress as valid. Were not the Americans rebelling against a foreign master rather than a legitimate indigenous ruler, just as the Dutch and Corsicans had done? Were not the battles of all three waged against overwhelming odds? And, in all three instances, were not the remaining European powers prepared to sit idly by and await the resolution of the conflict? Just as crucial to an understanding of Catherine's response to the American crisis was the outcome of the two precedents: had they not led, even when successful, to nothing more dramatic than a slight alteration in the balance of power? This would seem to have been the lesson of the past insofar as the empress was concerned.

Let us now turn to a closer examination of the all-important Corsican precedent, to which Catherine applied the terminology later employed by the Americans. Catherine's interest in the Corsicans and their heroic leader, General Pasquale Paoli, surfaced in the late spring of 1768, when she received word that the French government had purchased the rights to Corsica from Genoa. Dismayed, she promptly ordered her charge d'affaires in Venice, the Marquis de Maruzzi, to establish a secret channel of communications with Paoli, "ce defenseur de la liberte," as she termed him, to discover what his chances of success were. If they appeared promising, he was to pledge Russian arms and ammunition to the rebels.[3] To the British ambassador to St.

Petersburg, Nikita Panin disclosed the empress's concrete intention, should the findings prove positive: she proposed to dispatch to Corsica enough war material to equip seven thousand men. For this purpose she would require two British merchantmen, freighted ostensibly under private auspices in order to avoid unpleasantness with the French.[4] Britain's reluctance to extend itself militarily (the pacifist inclinations of Lords Bute and Bedford, Catherine complained) put a temporary damper on the project; but once the Turks declared war on Russia in the autumn of 1768, Catherine displayed renewed interest in Paoli and his colleagues, and with good reason. The Russian fleet was to be dispatched around the north of Europe, through the English channel and on into the Mediterranean to do battle with its Turkish counterpart, and Corsica might well prove useful as a supply point for the fleet. In a letter addressed "aux braves Corses, défenseurs de leur patrie et de la liberté," Catherine promised the rebels Russian funds to continue their struggle against the French. To her chargé in Venice she was more explicit in her motivation: noting that for some time she had viewed "avec admiration les efforts courageux de cet intrépide républicain [Paoli] pour sustraire sa nation au joug que l'injustice et l'ambition veulent lui imposer," she went on to order Maruzzi to seek to have Corsican ports put at the disposal of her fleet in return for Russian funds. Perhaps the island's Greek inhabitants, who were presumably longing for revenge against the Turks, might even agree to serve in the fleet.[5] Her plans were stymied; for, unbeknown to the empress, the island had already fallen to the French army of occupation, and Paoli had fled. The best the empress could now do for her republican friends was to resettle some of the Corsican refugees in the Crimea once that peninsula came under Russian hegemony in 1783.

Quite naturally, Catherine's enthusiasm for "cette petite république," as she labelled it, was far from disinterested: for aid to Paoli was projected first and foremost as a means to strike at the power and influence of France, Russia's chief antagonist in international affairs. Once the Ottoman Porte declared war on Russia at France's instigation, the island assumed even greater significance in Catherine's eyes. Thus, we may conclude that Corsica's war for independence was viewed by the empress as an ideologically neutral event, one that, however, acquired political significance within the specific context in which it was being waged. Accordingly, the crucial distinction between the Dutch and Corsican insurrections lay in the fact that Russia had no direct interest at stake in the former case, whereas it was very much concerned with France's threatening presence in the Mediterranean. By the same token, the crucial distinction between the Corsican and American insurrections, as we shall see, lay in the fact that the former struck at the very basis of French rather than British authority: France was Russia's "natural enemy," to resort to the parlance of the time, Britain—its "natural ally." Political considerations rather than ideological ones thus dictated that the empress take a dimmer view of the American revolt than the Corsican.

If this cursory examination of the larger political framework in which Catherine II evaluated the War for American Independence reveals that her judgments concerning the justice of the struggle were in no way expressed within the presumed context of direct Russian-American interaction, but rather that of Russian relations with Britain, then by extrapolation the struggle conveyed little direct meaning to the empress outside this framework. Yet one may not therefore simply assume that she condemned the War for American Independence on political rather than ideological grounds. For entering into her evaluation of the Anglo-American contest was an interpretation of the cause of the breach and a perception of the methods pursued by the British in their attempt to close it, that heavily colored her response to the events. To that interpretation we now turn.

In order to clarify Catherine II's perception of the War for American Independence we must first review her attitude toward the British nation, its king, and its foreign and domestic policies. It is in this area that we find some surprises. With regard to the British nation Catherine's verdict was unequivocally favorable. To some extent this may be attributed to a very personal consideration: in her hour of need as Grand Duchess, she had been lent secret service funds by British ambassador Sir Charles Hanbury-Williams to tide her through a crisis. This act she never forgot. But larger reasons of state also influenced her attitude. Throughout her lifetime Britain had served as a counterpoise to Russia's Bourbon enemies, and thus had preserved the precious balance of power. Their shared commercial interests contributed further to Catherine's classification of Britain as a natural ally. The absence of common borders and conflicting political interests heightened the significance of Britain for Russia. As the empress herself described the relationship in 1773, it had flourished because "our political views and interests are very closely interrelated, and lead by one path to the same goal."[6] Such unequivocal statements pervade Catherine's instructions to her diplomatic agents abroad right down to the eve of the American war.

It was not merely to the British nation as a personal or diplomatic consideration that the empress was attracted. For she esteemed the delicately balanced system of British government which, she agreed with Montesquieu, had rendered the nation the freest in the world. Nor was this analysis based upon a misunderstanding of its government: British minister to St. Petersburg, James Harris, after having discussed at length this system with the empress, came away convinced that she was "most perfectly mistress of our laws and constitution." Much of her knowledge stemmed from Blackstone, whose precepts she had mastered more thoroughly than Harris himself, the latter reported.[7] Aside from their elucidation of the laws, Catherine admired the manner in which the British wrote their history (Robertson) and their fiction (Sterne). She thought highly of all the inhabitants of the British Isles, in fact, purporting to see in the sober, industrious population precisely those qualities she wished to instill in her own subjects. Reflective of these desirable qualities was the Anglican Church, for which she shared a reverence with her numerous philosophe correspondents. Thanks in part to its spirit of toleration, the people themselves had been nurtured in toleration. In sum, the empress was, by her own admission, an "anglomaniac."

Catherine's affection for the British nation and people did not, however, extend to the king and his ministers. Her disdain for them originated at the close of the Seven Years' War, when George III ascended the throne and inserted Lord Bute into office, edging aside an embittered William Pitt. The new ministry proceeded to negotiate Britain's lucrative exit from the war, abandoning its Prussian ally to its fate. This act Catherine condemned as both immoral and unwise.[8] Her negative opinion was buttressed by Frederick II of Prussia, whose disgust over the policies of Bute and Bedford, who had actually negotiated the peace of Paris, he trumpeted all over Europe. The Russian and Prussian rulers agreed that constancy was the hallmark of a good ally, and in this respect they found Britain wanting. Its apostacy would not soon be forgotten. Exacerbating Catherine's distrust of British foreign policy was her dreary experience in attempting to conclude alliances with successive ministries. Convinced of Britain's invulnerable insular position, these ministeries until 1775 rebuffed all propositions to enter into formal continental connections.

This irritating policy of isolation, exclusive reliance upon sea power and of placing imperial interests above all others irked the empress and her director of foreign affairs (just as it had irked other Russian rulers as far back as Ivan IV). They were dismayed in particular by the king's tendency to shift the topic of negotiation to trade whenever that of political alliance was raised. And when the topic could not be avoided, or when the need became critical, the king's agents displayed a predictable desire to limit expenditures on foreign policy. "It is acceptable to handle merchandise in this manner," Panin angrily remarked, "and purchase it when one has need; but the English, permeated by the mercantile spirit, deceive themselves profoundly if they believe that one may act in a similar fashion with people."[9] Time and again we find Panin and the empress lamenting "la coutume anglaise de marchander comme des boutiquiers," "la policie marchande," and similar conduct.[10] The enthronement of mercantile values, if pressed too far, would lead to the downfall of powerful nations, as Montesquieu had warned: the United Provinces was a case in point.

Such complaints had been endemic to the history of Anglo-Russian relations. But in her more irritable moods the empress espoused a much more dramatic explanation for such dishonorable policies from a nation she had grown accustomed to revere. At his accession to the throne, the king had brought with him his favorite, John Stuart, Earl of Bute, who was alleged to be his mother's lover. Through this connection Catherine deduced that Bute was manipulating the king for his own obscure purposes.[11] The "influence" and "corruption" that the British Opposition claimed to identify as dominant elements were perceived by the Russian empress as well to be crucial to an understanding of British politics. Even after Bute had been forced from office, Catherine persisted in believing that he was the power behind the throne. It was a neat theory. It accounted for the otherwise unaccountable. And it did so by catering to the eighteenth-century fear of conspiracy. Thus, the crown was the helpless victim of the machinations of a favorite rather than the architect of the evil.[12]

As is evident, Catherine's perspective of British politics mirrored that of the Opposition in its general outlines.

Unable to comprehend dissension as an integral feature of a developing pluralistic society, and struck by its extent in this contentious period of British history, the empress concluded that the Opposition was correct: George III's advisors were intent upon upsetting the precarious balance among the crown, aristocracy and people so painstakingly established by the Glorious Revolution. Given enough time, Catherine decided, the crown, consciously or not, would eventually succeed in subverting the British Constitution, one of the finest ever evolved.[13] Curiously, then, the adherents to the Opposition appeared in the Russian autocrat's eyes not as dangerous malcontents, but as jealous guardians of tradition attempting to preserve a hallowed form of government in danger of corruption.

To some extent the empress had acquired her suspicions of the king and his ministers over the course of her observations of the conduct of British foreign policy. Frederick the Great's well-publicized accusations doubtless also had their impact. But the empress's convictions were perpetuated by the pronouncements of the members of the British Opposition themselves. These manifestoes were assiduously fed her by her ministers to the Court of St. James, who never failed to add their own commentaries. Three successive Russian ministers—Aleksandr Romanovich Vorontsov, Aleksei Semonovich Musin-Pushkin and Ivan Grigor'evich Chernyshev—were accused by the British government, with some justification, of displaying bias against the ruling ministry and in favor of the Opposition. Worried British ministers to St. Petersburg detected the nefarious influence of the Russian agents in London, and their own dispatches home reflected the quandary in which the Opposition had placed them. Lord Cathcart, for example, felt obliged in 1771 to observe that the empress "honours and loves the [British] nation, she pities the king, and has a low, not to say worse opinion of his ministers." Cathcart explained Catherine's proclivity in the following manner:

93

> The empress and her ministers have always been and still are, with respect to English politics, in the Opposition. We owe it, and many other misfortunes, to the animosity of some great men among ourselves, who are out of employment, and to the effort, their dependents use to vilify the measures of the present administration, and to set up opposite systems, which they declare to be theirs, and to be followed, were they in power. Such companions the late ambassador [Count Chernyshev] frequented in England, and such correspondence he is said still to hold. The picture he made of men and things, both from London and since his return, and the opinions, I am told he professes, on all occasions, show the school in which he has been trained, and that the pains taken with him have not been lost.

Of the conduct of Musin-Pushkin, Chernyshev's predecessor and successor, the minister could not be certain; "but I should suspect he corresponds with the sentiments of his court, and does not neglect those, who profess themselves friends, and advocates for northern alliances, and that of Russia in particular, and know they are considered as such here." Cathcart concluded his dispatch with an identification of the person he held most responsible for the undermining of Britain's relations with Russia: William Pitt, by this time the Earl of Chatham.[14]

Catherine had long harbored an admiration for Pitt, perhaps stemming back to her association with Hanbury-Williams, the ambassador who had supplied her with the secret service funds.[15] She could readily sympathize with his unbounded desire to destroy French power, a desire that had been thwarted by the entrance of Bute on the political stage. His denunciations of the base negotiations that had excluded Prussia, and of a peace treaty arranged by Bedford that relinquished too many hard-earned conquests, thus wounding rather than crippling France, struck a responsive chord with the empress. The ministerial instability so evident in British government following Pitt's fall from power persuaded the empress that only the Great Commoner possessed the popularity, authority and program sufficient to re-establish British prestige.[16] But Pitt's preachings were brought down to the concrete level for the empress by his insistence upon the necessity of forming a triple alliance composed of Britain, Prussia and Russia, to act as a counterbalance to Bourbon military strength left intact by the Peace of Paris.[17] Judging from surviving published letters, Pitt had not been at all reticent about sharing his hopes—in effect his promise for the future—with at least one Russian minister, a fact that did not escape the detection of the ministry.[18] Through Pitt and his followers, then, Catherine received her impressions of British politics.

As the North ministry became bogged down in the War for American Independence, Catherine discovered no reason to alter her evaluation of the British political scene. If anything, the American crisis confirmed her in her attitude. She was generally aware of the controversy surrounding the outbreak of war.[19] Lacking familiarity with the specific issues at stake in the contest, she simply borrowed that analysis most congenial to her own outlook—that of Pitt. In the dispatches of Musin-Pushkin she read of Pitt's fulminations against the Stamp Act and the Townshend duties, and of his excoriation of the Coercive Acts. And she could not help but be impressed with his assertion that "my whole system for America...is to secure to the colonies property and liberty."[20] Who could argue with such a platform? Who could perceive the horns of the dilemma upon which Pitt was caught? For Pitt's oppositon to the war bore little resemblance to that of the Rockingham Whigs, who applauded the colonists' struggle for independence, and even toasted George Washington. Rather, Pitt based his attack on the inability of the North ministry to deal with a potentially resolvable crisis. He advocated compromise. Who could foretell that his program of opposition both to North's policy of military suppression and the Whig's response of American independence was inadequate, that there was no viable third alternative, to be effected by a change of ministers? Who, in sum, could predict that the contradiction between the Declaratory Act of 1766 and the Declaration of Independence one decade later was irresolvable? Certainly not Catherine II, who took Pitt as her guide. Until the decisive battle at Yorktown shattered them, she persevered in her hopes that a more reasonable British ministry would make the concessions vital to the return of the rebellious colonies to their original allegiance. Like Pitt, she sought peace for North America, not independence; for only a negotiated settlement under a more amenable ministry would enable Britain to resume its customary role as chief bulwark to French revanchist tendencies.

Given the outlook she had borrowed from Pitt, it is scarcely surprising to find the empress rejecting decisively persistent British appeals for military assistance in the struggle with the colonies.[21] After all, responsibility for the crisis lay with successive British administrations, and North's in particular, and not with the insurgents, Catherine had determined. The colonists' grievances, voiced in Europe by Benjamin Franklin and Silas Deane, were justified. The Americans had been "provoked" into resistance, a fact the North ministry might have recognized, had it not been so preoccupied with mere survival.[22] Scorning the liberality essential to compromise, Lord North had resorted to the unwarranted and counterproductive application of force. This was not the way to handle the rupture, as Catherine never tired of pointing out to British diplomats in St. Petersburg. A reversal of policy was called for: it was incumbent upon the king to propose conciliatory measures. If he failed to do so, he risked alienating the colonists completely, and perhaps losing them altogether and forever (a prediction the empress now also applied to Ireland). By failing to display moderation, moreover, the king and his ministry were alienating the British public, for according to the empress the measures his Majesty's ministers had adopted, and were pursuing, were far from enjoying the approbation of the nation in general.[23]

Catherine was anxious to see a compromise because she had so little faith that the colonies could be recaptured solely by force: in April 1777, for example, British chargé d'affaires Richard Oakes, in discussing the inroads made by the Opposition viewpoint at court, noted "a readiness of giving credit to such disadvantageous reports has lately increased here; and I have reason to believe, that even those here, who wish us the best, look upon the reduction of our colonies to obedience as an effort of the utmost difficulty, and of very doubtful issue."[24] Force in fact would produce the very opposite result: it would reinforce American determination to break free of the mother country. And the prospect of a Great Britain shorn of its most flourishing possessions did not in the least enthrall the empress: "Je souhaite de tout mon coeur que mes amis, les anglois, s'accomodent avec leurs colonies," she noted in 1775. But such an eventuality she did not deem likely: "tant de mes prophèties se sont accomplies," she complained, "que je crains de voir l'Amèrique se dètacher de l'Europe de mon vivant."[25] This sense of impending disaster permeated all her comments on Britain's efforts to reconquer its colonies. One year after voicing her original fears, she was no more optimistic about the outcome of the war: "Que dites-vous de ces colonies qui disent adieu à jamais à l'Angleterre?" she inquired of the same correspondent. To this rhetorical question she provided her own response in the form of another question: "N'y a-t-il pas là de quoi ranger tout le monde du côtè de l'Opposition?"[26] As this last passage indicates, blame for the deteriorating situation had to be placed squarely at the doorstep of George III and his ministry.

The calamitous defeat of Burgoyne at Saratoga in the autumn of 1777 confirmed Catherine's worst fears: now Britain would have to arrange the most acceptable peace it could, one that would almost certainly entail something approaching total independence.[27] No degree of force could rectify the mistakes of the past; and to continue the war would be to court total defeat. But rather than grow more pliable in the face of adversity, the North ministry grew more rigid, and apparently more oblivious to the justified attacks of the Opposition. Thanks to this obstinacy, the British nation was saddled with an administration that could neither win the war on the field of battle nor lose it gracefully at the conference tables. For the loss of their possessions, with an accompanying plummet from the heights of international prestige and power, the British people could blame no one but the King and his ministry. What Molière had put into the mouth of George Dandin, Catherine II directed angrily to the king: "Tu l'a bien voulu."[28]

The empress had not only adopted the Opposition's interpretation of the causes of the War for American Independence, she had seen her convictions strengthened by the criticism the conduct of this same war had spawned. Musin-Pushkin and, after 1779, Ivan Matveevich Simolin, her ministers to London, catered to her view of the war by meticulously priming her with the broadsides of the Opposition, which she eagerly perused. This constant flow of literature served to sustain the empress's negative evaluation of British policies and politicians. To British ministers now attempting to negotiate treaties of alliance with Russia, this literature appeared subversive. At one point Harris bemoaned "the virulence and inconsiderate conduct of Opposition," while three years later Aleksei Grigor'evich Orlov, brother of the former favorite, noted to him that Catherine's great misfortune "was believing in the Opposition." The empress, he lamented, has received her impressions of George III and his administration from "printed speeches and newspaper trash." These writings had shaped her outlook, and jaundiced her view of the prevailing system in Britain. "In this My Lord," Harris concluded his dispatch, "I am unfortunately confirmed by every action of her life. And as this error is rooted in strong prejudice, though the last it will be the most

98

difficult to remove."[29] The same diagnosis Harris had occasion to hear time and again, not only from the empress but from her (and his) trusted confidant, Prince Potemkin, who held the "language of the Opposition, disapproving of our conduct, and condemning our military operations."[30] These assessments the British minister presumably heard with some measure of embarassment as well as with displeasure; for he himself was counted among the Whig Opposition. In such fashion were Britain's efforts to attain a Russian alliance paralyzed by political dissent within Great Britain itself.

Catherine's disapproval of Britain's conduct of the war in North America, like that of the Opposition, at times extended beyond mere fear of ignominious military defeat. Especially when she was provoked by incomprehensible British policies, she resorted to the theory that the king and his ministers—for the empress no longer placed the blame for Britain's tragic position on ill-intentioned favorites, but by the latter part of the 1770s espied an actual conspiracy between the king and his ministers—were seeking to take advantage of the dislocations created by the war to upset the traditional balance between the various elements of government. By purchasing elections to Parliament, by suborning members and by persecuting the Opposition in the name of national unity, they were bent upon asserting royal tyranny. The prolongation of the war in North America was interpreted by Catherine as a contributory factor in the corruption of the democratic element in British government by the executive (a constant danger in mixed forms of government): "Il falloit ne point provoquer leas Américains, pour faire pencher la balance du côté du roi (souverain), en un mot comme cent," she complained.[31] By process of extrapolation, Britain's liberties were at stake in America, and America's in Britain. Pitt had been absolutely correct in his prognosis. Unhappily for the British nation, it had lost its greatest leader to death just when it had greatest need of him.[32]

Pitt's direst predictions, and Catherine's, seemed to have materialized in December 1781, with the arrival in St. Petersburg of news that Cornwallis had been compelled to surrender at Yorktown. Now not only was the possibility of a military solution to the American imbroglio obviated, but reconciliation was also eliminated. Total independence for the former colonies was now inevitable. As was the case from the very outbreak of hostilities, Catherine was merciless in her judgment of her natural ally. Wrote the disconsolate Harris: "They attribute the loss we have sustained to our misconduct, and instead of expressing that degree of concern and allarm a nation whose interests are so indiscriminately connected with those of England, ought to feel, they exclaim against us in the most unconditional manner." Potemkin was somewhat more sympathetic, but interspersed his sorrow with a "great portion of illiberal blame."[33] No one at court had a kind word for British policy. Thanks to the greed and stupidity of the king and his ministers, the most desirable of all colonial possessions had been flung away. The loss was both devastating and irreparable. The sole redeeming feature of the outcome was the downfall of the North cabinet and the salvation of British liberty. But this liberty had been redeemed at a stiff price.

When in July of 1779 Catherine had proposed that the British make peace by ceding partial liberty to the Americans, and Harris had retaliated with the inquiry as to her own reaction if a foreign power had suggested that she take a similar step, her response was blunt: "J'aimerais mieux perdre ma tête."[34] Such was still her verdict eight years later, when another British minister, Alleyne Fitzherbert who had served as British negotiator at the Paris peace talks, loyally sought to mitigate the consequences of his king's policies by insisting that the loss of the former colonies was really a blessing in disguise. The empress, outraged at this feeble effort to exculpate the perpetrator of what she condemned as a state crime, retaliated by expressing the hope that the Good Lord might spare her such a blessing. Had she considered herself responsible for the sacrifice of a single of the "fifteen [sic] colonies," she vowed, "je me serois brulé la cervelle d'un coup de pistolet."[35] Here was the ruthless verdict of an empress who had witnessed her treasured ally squander away an empire.

Conspicuously absent from Catherine's verdict was any condemnation of the Americans for their resistance to British authority. She in fact admitted that their actions were justified, if harmful from the point of view of Russian foreign policy. She was indignant that George III had permitted the situation to deteriorate to the point where separation became unavoidable. For several years after the outbreak of war she had clung to the hope that some form of conciliation might prove possible. When this hope was revealed as groundless, she steeled herself to the independence of the colonies, and heaped even more scorn upon the responsible actors. But there she let matters rest. Once the colonies actually procured their independence, Catherine ceased to take any further interest in them at all, for the damage had been done.

There could be no question of an ideological threat emanating from the new republic any more than from the Dutch republic or Corsica. Were not the empress and the American rebels in fact inspired by the same interpretation of British politics, an interpretation most lucidly and convincingly espoused by William Pitt, the hero of two continents? Evocative terms such as "liberty," "independence" and "republic" were as prevalent in Catherine's vocabulary as in that of the Americans, or the British Opposition for that matter. How was the empress to perceive that the Americans were imparting new meanings to traditional terms?[36] How was she to foresee that the next political entity to employ the terminology would be not another outlying area controlled by a distant metropolis, but a sovereign nation casting aside its own political traditions? That she could not does not imply myopia on her part. Her failure rather indicates that she was deriving her judgments from the framework of her times, a framework just as congenial to those she accepted as her intellectual peers—Frederick the Great and William Pitt—as it was to herself. Not until the storming of the Bastille in 1789 would the empress be forced to re-examine her understanding of the terms employed by the American revolutionaries, and of the American Revolution itself. But this reinterpretation of the past is another story entirely, and historians must not permit their awareness of the events of 1789 to color their perceptions of the events of 1776.

## NOTES

1. For some examples of Western historical writing see Michael T. Florinsky, *Russia: A History and an Interpretation* (New York: Macmillan, 1974), I, 511; John C. Hildt, "Early Diplomatic Negotiations of the United States with Russia," in *Johns Hopkins University Studies in Historical and Political Science*, 24, Nos. 5 and 6 (1906), 18; Melvin C. Wren, *The Western Impact Upon Tsarist Russia* (Chicago: Holt, Rinehart and Winston, 1971), p. 106; G.P. Gooch, *Catherine the Great and Other Studies* (Hamden, Conn.: Archon Books, 1966), p. 95; Eufrosina Dvoichenko-Markova, "The American Philosophical Society and Early Russian-American Relations," *Proceedings of the American Philosophical Society*, 94, No. 6 (1950), 554; Charles Larivière, *Catherine II et la Revolution francaise d'après de nouveaux documents* (Paris: Le Soudier, 1895), pp. 59-60; Paul Fauchille, *La diplomatie francaise et la Ligue des Neutres de 1780* (Paris: G. Pedone-Lauriel, 1893), p. 58; Carl Bergbohm, *Die bewaffnete Neutralität 1780-1783* (Berlin: Puttkammer and Muhlbrecht, 1884), p. 59; Erwin Hoelzle, *Russland und Amerika* (Munich: R. Oldenbourg, 1953), p. 29. According to Fauchille, Henri Doniol (*Histoire de la participation de la France à l'éstablissement des États-Unis d'Amérique*, 5 vols. [Paris: Imprimerie Nationale, 1884-1892]) and Voltes-Bou ("La tradición juridica del Consolat del Mar y la Neutralidad Armada de Catalina II de Rusia," *Documentos y Estudios. Instituto Municipal de Historia*, 4 [1961], 9-51), only French diplomatic intervention prevented the Empress from entering the lists against the Americans, whereas Miecislaus Haiman *(Poland and the American Revolutionary War* [Chicago: Polish Roman Catholic Union of America, 1932]) insists Polish complications accomplished this end (p. 3). For Soviet writing See A. I. Startsev, "Amerikanskii vopros i russkaia diplomatiia v gody voiny SShA za nezavisimost'," in *Mezhdunardnye sviazi Rossii v XVII-XVIII vv.*, ed. L.G. Beskrovnyi (Moscow: Nauka, 1966), p. 468; Startsev, "V. Franklin i russkoe obshchestvo XVIII veka," *Internatsional'naia literatura*, Nos. 3-4 (1940), p. 215; Startsev, "F. V. Karzhavin i ego amerikanskoe puteshestvie," *Istoriia SSSR*, No. 3 (1960), p. 139; V. I. Rabinovich, *S gishpantsami v Novyi Iiurk i Gavanu (Zhizn' i puteshetsvie F. V. Karzhavina)* (Moscow: Mysl', 1967), p. 20; G. P. Makogonenko, *Nikolai Novikov i russkoe prosveshchenie XVIII veka* (Moscow-Leningrad: Khudozhestennaia Literatura, 1961), pp. 384-85. It would serve no purpose to cite Soviet sources *ad infinitum*, for they all mirror the same misconcieved image of a polarity in eighteenth-century political thought and practice. We might, however, note that the most authoritative Soviet works on the subject, *Stanovlenie russko-amerikanskikh otnoshenii, 1775-1815* (Moscow: Nauka, 1966), and *Rossiia i voina SShA za nezavisimost' 1775-1783*

(Moscow: Mysl', 1976) (the latter translated into English by C. Jay Smith with the title *Russia and the American Revolution* [Tallahassee, Florida: The Diplomatic Press, 1976]), by N. N. Bolkhovitinov, are somewhat more cautious. In the former Bolkhovitinov notes "the class antagonism of the tsarist government, and especially Catherine II herself, toward the rebellious American" (p. 87, and see also pp. 59-60); but subsequently (pp. 91-92) attempts to come to grips with the facts by acknowledging that "in principle" Catherine feared and hated the Americans and their revolution, whereas "in practice" it failed to elicit from her an ideological response. In the second work he pursues this interpretation: "In principle, of course, the War of the American Revolution of 1775-1783 and the French Revolution of 1789-1794, as phenomena similar in character, provoked a sharply negative reaction from the ruling classes, both of Russia, and also of other feudal-absolutist states. But this was only in principle. In practice, by virtue of concrete objective reasons and circumstances...the general international situation added up very favorably for the United States (in contradistinction to France)" (p. 229 in the Russian edition, p. 183 in the English). While perhaps a defensible thesis, it does not reveal much about the empress's intellectual outlook or response to the American Revolution. For a bibliographic survey of Soviet writings on this theme, see my "Soviet Views of Early Russian-American Relations," *Proceedings of the American Philosophical Society,* 116, No. 2 (1972), 148-56.

2. See my "Nikita Panin, Russian Diplomacy and the American Revolution," *Slavic Review,* 28, No. 2 (1969), 12.

3. Nikita Panin to the Marquis de Maruzzi, 11 October 1768, published in *Sbornik imperatorskago russkago istoricheskago obshchestva,* 87 (1893), 165-66. (This most important of pre-Revolutionary historical serials, which published much of Catherine's diplomatic correspondence through 1777, as well as a significant number of her private letters, will hereafter be referred to as *SIRIO.*)

4. Cathcart to Weymouth, 12/23 October 1768, in ibid., 12 (1873), 388-89. For additional traces of Catherine's interest in Paoli, see her letters, to Voltaire of 6/17 December 1768 (where she remarks that he "sait combattre pour ses foyers et son indépendance"), in ibid., 10 (1872), 309, and to I. G. Chernyshev, her ambassador to London, cited in S. M. Solov'ev, *Istoriia Rossii s drevneishikh vremen,* Book 14 (Moscow: Mysl' 1965), 316.

5. Letter to Maruzzi in *SIRIO,* 87: 438, 445-46, and to the Corsicans in 10:342-43. For additional letters see ibid., 1(1867), 20; 10:337; 12:431; 87:436-38; and 143 (1913), 43.

6. Cited in ibid., 118 (1904), 473; see also ibid., 135 (1911), 235 for the same statement one year later. For Catherine's attraction to the British nation in general, see ibid., 10:62, vol. 12:209 and 342 ("J'aime

mes allies naturels, et...j'estime cette nation"), vol. 48 (1885), 388, vol. 118:454, and vol. 140 (1912), 35.

7. The Third Earl of Malmesbury, ed., *Diaries and Correspondence of James Harris, First Earl of Malmesbury,* 2nd ed. (London: Robert Bently, 1845), I, 199 (3 June 1779). For Catherine's infatuation with Blackstone (although she did not believe his lessons to be directly applicable to Russia), see *SIRIO,* 23 (1878), 52 ("Oh, ses commentaires et moi, nous sommes inseparables" she wrote in August 1776), 57, 66, 92, and 159; for a recent study of Catherine's extensive personal observations upon reading Blackstone, see Marc Raeff, "The Empress and the Vinerian Professor: Catherine II's Projects of Government Reforms and Blackstone's Commentaries," *Oxford Slavonic Papers,* NS 7(1974), 18-41.

8. Frank Spencer in his "The Anglo-Prussian Breach of 1762: An Historical Revision" (*History,* 41 [1956], 100-12) argues that Great Britain did not abandon Prussia in 1762, but rather Frederick II dreamed up the story to suit his own purposes. His point seems strained, especially in the light of the correspondence of the Russian minister to London after having discussed the Prussian affair with Bute in early 1762 (see *SIRIO,* 37 [1883], 174-76). Regardless of the truth of the matter, this paper is concerned with what Catherine perceived to be the truth rather than the actual course of events.

9. Cited in *SIRIO,* 87:300.

10. Cited in F. de Martens, *Récueil des traités et conventions conclus par la Russie avec les puissances étrangères,* IX (St. Petersburg: Ministerstvo Putei Soobshcheniia, 1892), 225; see also the dispatch of the Danish resident Berger, 1/12 June 1775, in Rusland, Depescher, no. 275 (papers housed in the Royal Danish Archives, Copenhagen) and *SIRIO,* 87:330 and 349.

11. Both Bute and Bedford the empress suspected of pro-French sympathies; she apparently arrived at her suspicion on the basis of dispatches fom her minister in Britain: see, for example, ibid., 48:214 (from A. R. Vorontsov, 5/16 November 1762); see Panin's dispatches to I. G. Chernyshev in 1768 and 1769 in ibid., 87:116-17 and 299, and Lord Cathcart's report of 1771 in vol. 19 (1876), 230.

12. This was a widespread theory, shared even by American Whigs; see Bernard Bailyn, *The Ideological Origins of the American Revolution* (Cambridge, Mass: Harvard University Press, 1967), p. 128.

13. Blackstone has written in his Commentaries that there had to be one "supreme irresistable, absolute, uncontrolled authority, in which the jura summi imperii, or the rights of sovereignty reside," and located this in Parliament. Catherine accepted this analysis as suitable to the British character. But her ministers to Great Britain frequently described the corruption rampant in Parliament: see for

105

instance the dispatch of A. S. Musin-Pushkin, 1768, in V. N. Aleksandrenko, *Russkie diplomaticheskie agenty v Londone v XVIII veke* (Warsaw: Varshavskii Uchebnyi Okrug, 1897), II, 124-28 (Catherine kept the dispatch seventeen months); for Catherine's worries in 1773, see *SIRIO,* 12:302. See also footnote 30 below.

14. Cited in *SIRIO,* 19:228-29. Catherine gave express orders to her agents in Britain to keep her up to date on the activities of the various parties (she used precisly the term party, or *partiia* in Russian): see for example her letter to I. G. Chernyshev, 1768, in ibid., 87:118, where she also orders him to keep on the good side of all the parties.

15. See her inquiry about Pitt in her letter to the British ambassador of 21 December 1756, in The Earl of Ilchester and Mrs. Langford-Brooke, editors and translators, *The Correspondence of Catherine the Great When Grand Duchess, with Sir Charles Hanbury-Williams and Letters from Count Poniatowski* (London: Thornton Butterworth Ltd., 1928), p. 252.

16. Minister to London A. S. Musin-Pushkin in July 1766 described Pitt to Catherine as "beloved, honored, imitated, and supreme *(vlasten)*": see Aleksandrenko, *Russkie diplomaticheskie agenty,* 1, 34n; for Catherine's fears once Pitt had fallen from power for the last time in 1768, see *SIRIO,* 10:202.

17. For an elucidation of the Northern System see my "The Rise and Fall of the Northern System: Court Politics and Foreign Policy in the First Half of Catherine II's Reign," *Canadian Slavic Studies,* 4, No. 3 (1970), 547-69.

18. Vorontsov was accused by Lord Sandwich of participating in Pitt's opposition, and of offering an unflattering picture of British foreign policy to his superiors: see I. Iu. Rodzinskaia, "Russko-angliiskie otnosheniia v shestidesiatykh godakh XVIII v.," *Trudy Moskovskogo Gosudarstvennogo Istorikoarkhivnogo Instituta,* 21 (1965), 256. Indeed, an unidentified member of Pitt's circle promised Vorontsov that Britain would act more generously toward Russia once Pitt came to power. And Pitt himself seemed to hold out to the minister the same prospect: he wrote to Vorontsov in March 1764 as the latter was on his way back home: "Je ne cesserai d'envisager comme une perte particulière et publique le départ d'un ministre si zélé pour l'harmonie parfaite de nos cours et pour cette union salutaire de puissances dans le Nord, qui seule puisse assurer le repos de l'Europe contre les vues dangereuses des confédérés du Sud" (letter published in P. I. Bartenev, ed., *Arkhiv Kniazia Vorontsova,* 29 (Moscow: Universitetskaia Tipografiia, 1883), 303-04, and for similar sentiments some five months later, see ibid., pp. 305-06. Pitt did of course come to power again in 1766, and Panin responded by reviving the Anglo-Russian treaty project (see *SIRIO,* 109 [1901], 206); but Pitt's mental condition left little opportunity for detailed attention to foreign affairs.

19. See the reports of dispatches (1775) concerning the American revolt being read in the State Council in I. Ia. Chistovich, ed., *Arkhiv Gosudarstvennago Soveta*, I, pt. 1 (St. Petersburg: E. I. V. Kantseliaria, 1869), 323-25.

20. Cited in Frank O'Gorman, *The Rise of Party in England: The Rockingham Whigs, 1760-1782* (London: Allen and Unwin, 1975), p. 335.

21. James Harris's constant rejections are splendidly described in Isabel de Madariaga, *Britain, Russia and the Armed Neutrality of 1780* (New Haven: Yale Univ. Press, 1962).

22. For revealing the truth about conditions in America, Catherine argued, Benjamin Franklin and Silas Deane should have been heeded instead of proscribed: see *SIRIO*, 27 (1880), 153-54; see also ibid., vol. 23:83, and the dispatch of the Danish chargé d'affaires, 30 July/10 August 1779, describing the caustic dispatches of Russian minister to London I. M. Simolin, in *Rusland, Depescher*, 1779, no. 6.

23. Blame for her "erroneous opinion" British ambassador Gunning placed on her ambassador to London, Chernyshev, and the opposition press, especially the St. James Chronicle: see *SIRIO*, 19, 504-05. Reports of Catherine's perusal of opposition pamphlets condemning the conduct of the war in North America are to be found in the dispatches of French minister Juigné, 1 and 15 October 1776, in Correspondence Politique: Russie, vol. 99, nos. 62 and 64, housed in the archives of the French Foreign Ministry, Paris (hereafter referred to as C.P.R., with appropriate volume and number). In the latter, the minister writes that the empress "regardoit les Américains commes rebelles; mais qu'elle trouvoit très maladroite la conduite tenue envers eux par le gouvernement anglois." Baron Grimm put the issue somewhat more colorfully in a letter to the empress in 1781, "C'est une étrange manie á papa George de croire qu'il pourra rentrer dans la maison des enfants après l'avoir incendiée six ans de suite": *SIRIO*, 33 (1881), 134. "There are moments when we must be too rigorous," Gunning reported having been warned by Catherine: see his letter to Suffolk of 31 August 1775, in ibid., 19:488. Force, she added, was not the suitable approach to deal with the problem.

24. Such attitudes, he feared, would deter the empress from entering into an alliance with Britain: see Oakes's dispatch of 7/18 April 1777, in State Papers, Foreign, vol. 91/101, no. 19, housed in the Public Records Office, London (hereafter referred to as S. P., with appropriate volume and number).

25. To Madam Bielke, in *SIRIO*, 27:44. She feared her predictions of eventual American independence would prove more accurate than the predictions of the medical faculty of the Sorbonne; see ibid., p. 29.

26. Ibid., p. 119.

27. By 1779 Russian minister to London Simolin was constantly reiterating the need for peace: see for example Danish chargé Schumacher's dispatch of 30 July/10 August 1779, in Rusland, Depescher, 1779, no. 6, and Corberon's of 10 September 1779, in C.P.R., vol. 103, no. 36 (repeating Prince Potemkin's complaint). For secondary accounts consult Isabel de Madariaga, *Britain, Russia and the Armed Neutrality,* esp. pp. 96-99, 251-54, and my own "Nikita Panin, Russian Diplomacy and the American Revolution," pp. 10-18. Unfortunately, complained Catherine, the king knew nothing but half measures; see *SIRIO,* 23:147.

28. Ibid., p. 146. Madame Bielke had dared suggest that the British Constitution was responsible for the dissension rending Parliament, to which Catherine remarked to Grimm that "ce n'est donc pas la forme, mes [sic] les acteurs qui sont fautifs" (ibid., vol. 23:92-93). And of course she reverted to her usage of the term "marchand drapier" ibid., pp. 137-38, 149 and 224), waxing especially sarcastic in the following passage: "O mon Dieu, mon Dieu! que de frères George partout, partout! que le bon Dieu bénisse les frères George, les bons citoyens et les Mittelmässige Passgänger, et puis raffolez du siècle et de ses productions!" (p. 192). The allusions are to the king's rigid middle class existence, and more particularly to his loyalty to his dim and ugly wife, by whom he had fifteen children. But of course Catherine was far from overjoyed at Burgoyne's defeat: "Je vous impose silence, de même qu'à moi, sur le grand spectacle de l'Amérique," she wrote to Baron Grimm 2 February 1778, "parce que l'existence est en contradiction avec la substance, le naturel avec le métier, l'âme avec le corps etc. etc. etc. Je ne veux plus entendre non plus parler de l'eritoire, de cette grand importante affaire, jusqu'à ce qu'elle soit arrivée" (pp. 78-79; see also pp. 73, 92-93, 147). According to Joseph II, the empress had told him during their meeting at Mogilev that "elle regrette dans son âme la mauvaise situation dans laquelle, à ce qu'elle croit, l'Angleterre se trouve, aimant les Anglais, mais méprisant la faiblesse du Roi et les sottises réiterees de leur ministère, qu'elle croit devoir succomber à ses facheuses circonstances, et elle en attend l'issue...." (A. R. von Arneth, ed., *Maria Theresia und Joseph II: Ihre Correspondenz* [Vienna: E. Gerolds Sohn, 1867], III, 268). He told the same to Harris: see the British minister's report of 14/25 July 1780 in Harris, *Diaries,* I, 280. As in almost every other respect, Catherine was in complete accord with Baron Grimm, who observed colorfully that "le procès la maman et les filles revêches est irracommodable et la maman l'a bien mèrite par sa rare et marbeilleuse sottise. S'il lui restait un grain de sagesse, elle dirait: Mes enfants, nous ne devons plus demeurer ensemble. Votre mère a été frappe d'aveuglement et a de quoi pleurer le reste de sa vie; mais oubliez le passé, et voyons si après avoir rompu notre mariage avec un scandale execrable, nous ne pouvons pas voisiner ensemble en

bonne intelligence" (to Catherine II, 17 September 1780, in *SIRIO,* 44 (1895), 112).

29. Harris to his father, 27 May 1778, in Harris, *Diaries,* I, 171. The conversation with Orlov is found in his letter to Stormont of 5/16 March 1781, in Foreign Office Papers, 65/2, no. 35 (these papers represent a continuation of the State Papers, and are also housed in the Public Records Office in London). For other traces of the empress's oppositionist views see Harris, *Diaries,* I, 272 and 395.

30. Harris to Stormont, 31 August/11 September 1781, in F.O. 65/4, no. 126. Even the empress's private secretary, A. A. Bezborodko, Harris found to be "tainted with a degree of those opposition principles I had observed so strongly to prevail in Prince Potemkin": F.O. 65/5, no. 186 (14/25 December 1781).

31. To an unidentified correspondent, 7 June 1778, in *SIRIO,* 27:153-54. In October of the same year she commented upon "ce parlement vendu" in a letter to Grimm (ibid., 23:102). Nor did the empress conceal her opinions from her fellow-monarch, Joseph II of Austria: "Je suis de l'avis de V. M. I. que, si le parlement d'Angleterre ne sers pas orageux à cette séance-ci, il n'y a plus rien à attendre de lui, mais il me semble qu'il voit broncher son gouvernement à chaque pas depuis vingt ans, et qu'il ne donne les guinées de la nation que pour faire payer à chaque individu l'approbation des fausses mesures du ministere": 7/18 December 1781, in A. R. von Arneth, ed., *Joseph II und Katharina von Russland: Ihr Briefwechsel* (Vienna: W. Braumüller, 1869), p. 116. Potemkin, as was to be expected, mirrored faithfully the empress's opinions, confiding to the French chargé that the English system was "inexplicable et qu'on ne pouvoit l'attribuer qu'au but que sembloit avoir George III d'étendre son pouvoir sur sa nation": Corberon to Vergennes, 10 September 1779, in C.P.R., vol. 103, no. 36. And as late as 1787, in conjunction with Britain's alliance with Prussia, she complained ironically of "fr. Ge, le défenseur de la liberté germanique, lui qui détruit celle de l'Angleterre" (*SIRIO,* 23:424).

32. Pitt died 11 May 1778, much to Catherine's chagrin. She wrote to Grimm: "Le mois de Mai m'a été très fatal: j'ai perdu deux hommes que je n'ai jamais vus, qui m'aimaient et que j'honorais—Voltaire et milord Chatham" (*SIRIO,* p. 93). The administration, she insisted, should have paid him more heed. And, influenced perhaps by Fox's dramatic speech, she denounced the way the government had allowed the pension to his designated heirs to fall into arrears: see ibid., pp. 102-03; and see also p. 122.

33. Harris, 7/18 December 1781, in F.O. 65/5, no. 182 (published with slight changes in Harris, *Diaries,* I, 415). The empress's disgust was both profound and longlasting. To Grimm she observed: "Mon frère le drapier [George III] éprouve les trente-six malheurs d'arlequin; il est beau après cela de ne pas succomber": *SIRIO,* 23:224; a month

later: "Je vous défends très expressèment de me parler jamais des galvadeurs de frère G. et de lui même aussi" (ibid., p. 227); and a little over two years later: "Ne me parlez pas de frère George, car jamais son nom ne fut nomme sans me bouillonner le sang" (ibid., p. 304).

34. Harris, *Diaries,* I, 217.

35. Le Comte [Phillippe-Paul] de Segur, *Mémoires ou souvenirs et anecdotes* (Paris: A. Eymery, 1825), III, 230. Segur's account coincides with that of the empress, who wrote to Grimm: "Oh! que les bons citoyens ont fait de mal à de certains pays! J'ai vu d'excellents citoyens perdre quinze provinces; Fitz Herbert soutient que c'est un vrai bondeur pour l'Angleterre. Que le ciel préserve tout honnête homme de ce bonheur": *SIRIO,* 23:395. The conversation obviously affected the empress, because seven months later she referred back to it, noting that she had no desire to experience the good fortune of the British king; for "il a perdu 15 provinces; je regarde cela comme un crime de lèse-état qui devrait être puni rigoureusement": ibid., p. 431; see also p. 435, where she notes she would not care to lose an inch of territory. Unable to erase the thought from her mind, she reverted to the theme in a discussion she held with her private physician, an Englishman: she asked him if his countrymen were still smiling over the loss of fifteen provinces, to which he rejoined that they had forgotten all about it. Retorted the empress: "There is no way one can forget about that" (17 November 1787, recorded in A. V. Khrapovitskii, *Dnevnik Khrapovitskogo* [St. Petersburg: A. F. Bazunov, 1874], p. 19).

36. The author of this paper is ill-equipped to follow the evolution of American republicanism from its traditional English Whig and radical roots, and will limit himself to the mention of several useful sources that relate to the topic. For the British background one may have recourse to Caroline Robbins, *The Eighteenth-Century Commonwealthmen: Studies in the Transmission, Development, and Circumstances of English Liberal Thought from the Restoration of Charles II until the War with the Thirteen Colonies* (Cambridge, Mass.: Harvard University Press, 1959). For the radical transformation of British thought by the colonists, consult Bernard Bailyn, *The Ideological Origins of the American Revolution,* and for the more practical application of this thought see the same author's *The Origins of American Politics* (New York: Knopf, 1967). One of the points the present paper seeks to make is that the Russian empress, like most onlookers, remained oblivious to the transformation of the traditional political framework and its terminology perpetrated by the American colonists.

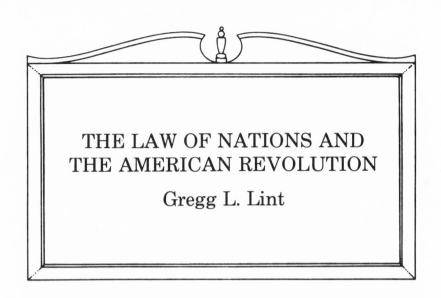

# THE LAW OF NATIONS AND THE AMERICAN REVOLUTION
## Gregg L. Lint

A conception of the law of nations lay at the heart of American foreign policy from the founding of the nation. The revolutionary leaders, in fact, postulated a new system of international relations—an American system—based on universal recognition of the law of nations and pointing toward the efforts of the Congress of Vienna. Without such a system the Americans' hopes for future neutrality and free trade were doomed to failure, and they could not guarantee the lasting peace that would permit establishment and expansion of the new nation's economic foundations so as to insure its survival in a hostile world.

The foreign policy conceived by the founding fathers had little place in the eighteenth century, with its ideas of unfettered sovereignty and limited sense of international interdependence. Perhaps for this reason, recent historians, even those who stress the important interplay between the intellectual, political, and economic orientations of the founding fathers, have paid insufficient attention to the importance of the concept of the law of nations for the country's early statesmen.[1] This has been unfortunate because, by its actions and example, the

This article has appeared in *Diplomatic History,* 1 (Winter 1977), 20-34. Reprinted by permission of the publisher.

United States did seek to use, modify or extend the existing law to meet both its immediate and long-range objectives.

On a philosophical plane Americans were drawn to the law of nations because of its origin in natural law and their attitude toward the rule of law in domestic society. According to authorities such as Grotius, Pufendorf, and Vattel, the law of nations was divided into two sets of rules: the necessary law that was synonomous with the law of nature and binding on all nations because of an intrinsic validity, and the stipulative law or law of treaties that was limited in its force to the signatories of a particular treaty. It was to the necessary law that Americans felt their initial and very genuine bond, for they were fond of referring to natural law as the foundation of their rights; indeed, they justified their independence according to the law of nature and nature's God. At the same time, Americans saw order as the necessary ingredient for civil society, and it was the rule of law that provided that order. It was not difficult to translate this belief in a rule of law from a society of men to one of states. The municipal law of civil society became the law of nations of world society.

Self-interest, as reflected in the desire for free trade and the need to protect and maintain the nation's sovereignty, also drew Americans to the law of nations. To Americans commercial and foreign policy were synonymous. Economics was the dominant force of international society. They sought to trade on an equal basis with all nations in both war and peace, but it was in time of war that their need for economic growth and prosperity could best be met. Neutrality was, therefore, their policy, and a system of accepted law to protect that neutrality their need. In addition, the United States was weak. The founding fathers, aware of that fact, sought to remove America from the maelstrom of European politics with its balance of power, large standing armies, and war as an instrument of national policy and to sanctify its position by a law of nations as set down in the works of the authorities and hopefully expanded by American efforts. They intended that the smallest republic be as respected and as sovereign as the greatest empire.[2]

The Treaty Plan of 1776 was the first step in the American policy and clearly reflected long-term American interests.[3] It proposed a commercial connection based on general freedom of trade except in contraband or to places blockaded or besieged in wartime, the acceptance of the doctrine that "free ships make free goods," and a definition of contraband favorable to the United States.[4] In both language and the attempt to establish neutral trade the Model Treaty was similar to the Anglo-Dutch treaty of 1674, which was the result of the British desire to take over the carrying trade opened up by the Franco-Dutch war then going on.[5] It was a commercial rather than a military alliance because the opening of American markets was seen as an adequate reward for aid extended to the United States.[6] John Adams, the principle author of the plan, declared that a commercial treaty with the United States would act as a repeal of the British navigation acts for France and was ample compensation for her aid and recogniton of American independence even if these actions should involve her in a war. He was adamant about his distaste for any political or military connection that "might embarrass us in after times and involve us in future European wars" and thus compromise the true policy of the United States, "perfect neutrality," and was heartened by the inability of certain members of Congress to compromise his plan by the inclusion of an entangling alliance, exclusive privileges, or the guaranty of possessions.[7]

Article XXVI of the Treaty Plan and Article I of the Anglo-Dutch treaty stated the principle of freedom of trade in almost the same words but differed in emphasis. The American plan referred to freedom of trade in terms of its unobstructed operation in time of war, while the treaty of 1674 spoke of a freedom established during peace that was not to be hindered by the outbreak of war. The American version more nearly met American needs because of the implication that war could not affect trade, even that opened up in wartime because of the demand for neutral carriers. In time of war, the nations without adequate navies, particularly France, would open to neutral carriers their colonial trade that in time of peace was generally limited to the mother country. If the principle noted above became widely accepted, a part of the necessary law of nations, it would explicitly legalize such trade and, even more importantly, would nullify the effect of the infamous Rule of 1756 by which Great Britain sought to prohibit such trade.[8]

In the Anglo-Dutch treaty of 1674 the principle of "free ships make free goods" was separated from the section dealing with the general freedom of commerce, while the Model Treaty placed the doctrine in the article dealing with unobstructed trade in wartime. The Dutch treaty implied that the principle was only part of the stipulative law of nations. The Model Treaty, however, by linking the two principles, attempted to modify the law because the right to freedom of trade was an accepted principle of the necessary law of nations, while that of "free ships make free goods" was not. If the prohibition of the seizure of enemy goods on neutral ships could be made part of the more accepted principle, it might also be seen as part of the necessary law of nations.

It is axiomatic that a nation contemplating neutrality should want as limited and as inclusive an enumeration of contraband goods as possible. The Model Treaty and the Anglo-Dutch treaty were almost identical in their definitions of contraband. Indeed, the similarity in language raises a question about American intentions, for the definition was not as liberal as might have been expected. It ignored the more limited provisions of the Anglo-Russian treaties of 1734 and 1766 (the second of which served as the source of the definition of contraband contained in the Armed Neutrality), and did not approxi-

114

mate later American efforts that tried to remove the designation of contraband altogether.[9] This failure to go to the limit can probably be attributed to a need to ground the American position on solid precedent and a desire to avoid anything that might appear radical to states that already saw the United States as a threat to the established order.

Had France accepted the Treaty Plan of 1776 as its sole connection with the United States, as ample reward for French aid, American long- and short-term objectives would have been met. France, however, demanded, and the United States by necessity was forced to accept, a treaty of alliance with a mutual and perpetual guaranty of possessions in the western hemisphere with no other condition set as a *casus foederis* than that war should break out.[10] Such an agreement had not been the intent of those who wrote the Model Treaty. Indeed, some Americans saw the French Alliance as a threat to the American character and to the gains that the United States had made and was making in the name of "true Republicanism."[11] The alliance was a problem, not because it tainted American policy by contact with the European system (although certainly some would have argued that it did), but because it threatened to undermine the long-term goals of the United States, to raise questions about the viability of American neutrality in any future war participated in by France, and because, if only by inference, it tied the destiny of the United States to the course of French foreign policy.

Moreover, the existence of the alliance made the United States reluctant to incur further obligations. John Adams was instructed, in the negotiation of a treaty with the Netherlands, to limit any alliance formed to the current war and to provide that there would be no separate peace. It was not to be an offensive treaty or contain any guaranty of possessions.[12]

The United States sincerely supported the principles of the Treaty Plan of 1776, the Treaty of Amity and

Commerce with France, and the later Armed Neutrality, but that did not mean that it could ignore its immediate interests while it pursued the long-range goal of providing a sound basis for future neutrality. American agents in Europe were instructed to adopt the ancient principle that "the goods and effects of enemies on board the ships and vessels of either party the United States and France, shall be liable to seizure and confiscation" should France not agree that "free ships make free goods."[13] This willingness to compromise an almost sacred rule was even clearer in a letter from the Committee on Foreign Affairs ordering its agents in Paris to press the French Government either to prohibit the carrying of British goods by French ships or allow American ships the right to "search into and make distinction between the bottom and the enemy's property conveyed in that bottom."[14]

Clearly, the United States supported the principle that "free ships make free goods" but did not always insist on it in fact. In 1778 American policy followed the strict law of nations, agreeing with it that the doctrine of "free ships make free goods" was part of the stipulative, rather than the necessary, law of nations. For example, a proclamation governing privateers issued in May 1778 ordered the observance of neutral rights but did not prohibit the seizure of enemy property on neutral ships.[15] As late as June 1780, after the initial declaration of the Armed Neutrality but before instructions from Congress could reach Europe, Benjamin Franklin declared the law in America to be settled: enemy property in the ship of a nation with whom the United States had no treaty could be seized under the provisions of the "old law of nations."[16]

The advent of the Armed Neutrality changed this policy. Its announcement laid down five principles: first, that neutral ships did have the right to trade freely from one port to another and on the coasts of the nations at war; second, that free ships did make free goods; third, that contraband would in the future be defined according to Articles X and XI of the Anglo-Russian treaty of 1766; fourth, that to be legal a blockade had to constitute a positive danger to any ships trying to enter the port; finally, that the four principles listed above should be the rule in all proceedings where a question existed concerning the legality of prizes.[17]

The first two of the points enumerated by Catherine in the declaration were already included in the commercial treaty with France; the fourth was not of immediate concern, and the fifth was merely a *pro forma* statement of the declaration's effect. The third of Catherine's points, the definition of contraband, was of the most interest to the United States. The Anglo-Russian treaty of 1766 stated, in Article X, that "with the single exception of warlike stores, the aforesaid subjects [of Great Britain and Russia] may transport to these places [not blockaded or besieged] all sorts of merchandise as well as passengers without the least impediment." Article XI then listed the "warlike stores" that could be seized.[18] There was no list, such as existed in the American Treaty of Amity and Commerce with France, of goods that could not be seized. The effect of this omission was to make the list of contraband inclusive and specifically to provide that anything not listed could not be seized. This provision removed a problem that generally existed when two lists, one of contraband and the other of noncontraband, existed side by side. In that case, the captor often seized the contraband together with anything not specifically listed as noncontraband. For the United States a provision such as that contained in the Anglo-Russian treaty of 1766 was clearly in its interest and was included in the treaty it signed with the Netherlands in 1783.[19]

The United States soon took action to bring its policy more into alignment with the principles of the Armed Neutrality. On 5 October 1780, Congress accepted the principles of the declaration, excepting only contraband as defined under the terms of the French treaty of 1778.[20] On 4 December 1781, that exception was modified by the adoption of a new ordinance on captures at sea that defined contraband according to the Anglo-Russian treaty of 1734.[21] Thus, to a significant degree it was the Armed Neutrality rather than the Treaty Plan of 1776 or the French treaty of 1778 that took the United States from the narrow confines of stipulative law to a broader application of the principles so obviously in its long-range interest.

To Catherine, the major objective of the Armed Neutrality was the advancement of Russia's position within the European system rather than neutral rights, but the American perception of her initiative made Catherine's motives largely irrelevant.[22] To Americans, the Armed Neutrality supported their interests and principles and was, in the words of one observer, "all that America would wish for on the subject" because ultimately the United States, as the world's greatest carrier and enjoying perpetual neutrality, would benefit the most from such an alteration in the established order.[23] Americans saw the Armed Neutrality not as a machination of traditional European politics but as an advance for the law, an effort finally to legislate "free ships make free goods" and a limited definition of contraband into the necessary law of nations. The founding fathers did not contest that such principles could be supported by the law of nature but that they were supported by a large number of nations, a sharp departure from contemporary thought on the origin of the law of nations. The reaction of the United States made it clear that American thought and action in regard to the law of nations, at least within the limited area of neutral rights, were becoming increasingly oriented toward the stipulative law as a dynamic force in the alteration of the law to meet its needs.

John Adams and Benjamin Franklin believed that the Armed Neutrality was an awakening of the European mind to the ideals and principles of the American Revolution and offered an opportunity to further the interests of the United States.[24] They proposed to liberalize the law of nations beyond what Catherine had seemed to indicate. John Adams wrote in April 1780 that

...as human reason advances, and men come to be more sensible of the benefits of peace, and less enthusiastic for the savage glories of war, all neutral nations will be allowed, by universal consent, to carry what goods they please in their own ships, provided they are not bound to places actually invested by an enemy.[25]

The implications of this statement for the law of nations were enormous; if adopted, such a principle would end any distinction between contraband and other goods or between the mother country and its colonies, bringing an absolute freedom of trade based not on treaty rights, but on the necessary law of nations. In June 1780 Benjamin Franklin proposed to remove even the distinction between neutral and enemy merchant ships when he argued that

...it is likely to become henceforth the law of nations, that free ships make free goods. England does not like this confederacy. I wish they would extend it still further, and ordain that unarmed trading ships, as well as fishermen and farmers; should be respected as working for the common good of mankind, and never interrupted in their operations, even by national enemies; but let only those fight with one another whose trade it is and who are armed and paid for that purpose.[26]

Both proposals were ultimately incorporated into American treaty-making efforts.

Americans supported the Armed Neutrality during and after the war because of what it contained and their hopes for its effect on the law of nations. In 1787 Thomas Jefferson stated that the pronouncements of the Armed Neutrality on "free ships make free goods" and contraband "may be considered now as the law of nations."[27] John Jay was instructed in 1794 to regulate blockades in accordance with the Armed Neutrality, and much of the debate over his treaty concerned the accomplishments of the League.[28]

119

The League of Armed Neutrality supported American ideals and attracted continuing interest because of its abstract principles that were seen as parts of the law of nations; but enthusiasm for a formal accession to its dictates by the United States waned and finally disappeared. During the war there was a certain incongruity in the United States, a belligerent, becoming part of a league to protect neutral rights. Nevertheless, Congress, on 5 October 1780, empowered its representatives abroad to support the League's principles and even accede to them.[29] John Adams did so in March 1781 when, after referring to the reformation of the maritime law of nations brought about by the American Revolution he stated, in a memorial to the States General of Holland, his wish that the United States become parties to it, "entitled to its benefits and subject to its duties."[30] His hopes were not realized, however, for an acceptance of the "duties" implied a willingness to act that did not exist. The Congress made this clear when, in June 1783, it declared that, while it was willing to recognize neutral rights in the final peace treaty, it would not accept any obligation to support them by force.[31] Finally, on 29 October 1783, Congress ordered that no further measures be taken to align the United States with the Armed Neutrality.[32]

The League of Armed Neutrality was a turning point in American foreign policy despite the fact that the United States never became a member. This is because the American refusal to join was not a rejection of the principles enunciated in Catherine's declaration or the precedents that, to Americans, it set for the future development of the law of nations, particularly in regard to neutral rights. Instead, the American decision of 1783 reflected the approach of peace and the reorientation of American policy toward long-term goals. The United States, therefore, rather than becoming a member of the League, set out to incorporate the League's principles, and lines of development for the law of nations implied by its very existence, into bilateral commercial treaties that would expand American commerce, establish a sound basis for future neutrality, and not involve it in the political affairs of Europe to the degree necessitated by membership in a European confederation of neutrals.

Between 23 January 1783 and 17 May 1786, the United States successfully negotiated treaties with the Netherlands, Sweden, and Prussia while failing to do so with Portugal, Denmark, and Great Britain. These efforts, whether successful or not, together with the French treaty of 1778 are important as showcases for the principles that the United States sought to establish and indicate the evolution of the American mind in which the distinction between the stipulative and necessary law of nations became increasingly blurred.

The cornerstone of any treaty negotiated by the United States was the doctrine that "free ships make free goods." It appeared in every negotiating proposal and final treaty through 1786 with the single exception of the abortive attempt to negotiate a treaty with Britain in April 1786.[33] The importance of the doctrine stemmed from the fact that, without it, the trading activities of the neutral state were limited to those things of its own produce that one or another belligerent might need or allow it to carry.

In regard to the right of the neutral nation to trade, the United States, for the first seven years of its existence, followed the policy set down in the Treaty Plan of 1776 of stating the doctrine of "free ships make free goods" and the inherent right of unobstructed trade in one article, while giving its necessary, if grudging, acceptance of the counterdoctrine that "enemy ships make enemy goods" in a separate article. That approach was followed in the treaties with France, the Netherlands, and Sweden.[34] This lack of innovation resulted from the fact that the provisions of the Treaty Plan of 1776 continued to meet American needs and were in line with the provisions of the Declaration of Armed Neutrality in the effort to make the principle of "free ships make free goods" part of the necessary law.

This changed on 20 December 1783, with the adoption of a revised treaty plan. From that date, the United States began a new effort to include the negative doctrine that "enemy ships make enemy goods" in the same article as the positive principle that "free ships make free goods" and the right of unobstructed trade.[35] This action decreased the visibility of the counterdoctrine, presaged the elimination of its presence altogether, and continued the American attempt to unite, in one article, all the provisions affecting the right of the neutral nation to trade freely in time of war. The policy was implemented in all later negotiations with Prussia, Denmark, Portugal, and Great Britain (the effort of 11 October 1785). The only departure came in the Prussian treaty and stemmed from the unwillingness of Prussia to acknowledge that neutral property on enemy ships was liable to seizure and resulted in the deletion of any mention of the principle that "enemy ships make enemy goods" from the treaty.[36] Though it had not proposed the elimination of the counterdoctrine to "free ships make free goods," the United States readily accepted the Prussian Position because it was a step in the direction of a new principle: neutral goods should be free on whatever ship they were found.

The development of the American position on the definition of contraband is also important. Initially the United States followed traditional designations of contraband and noncontraband goods, but this policy changed in January 1783 with the ratification of the treaty with the Netherlands. That treaty contained an enumeration of contraband goods but not a list of those that were not contraband, thus giving the clear implication that the list of contraband was inclusive and that everything not appearing on it was noncontraband and could not be seized.[37] This indicated that the United States was committed to the definition contained in the third article of the Declaration of the Armed Neutrality, for the Dutch treaty defined contraband in essentially the same terms as did the Anglo-Russian treaty of 1766.

On 20 December 1783, with the adoption of the revised treaty plan, the United States began an effort to liberalize the law as it applied to contraband even further—to go beyond what had appeared in the Declaration of the Armed Neutrality. The United States removed any real definition, declaring that to prevent further controversy it would, in effect, allow the belligerent to seize, within reason, any article considered contraband as long as compensation was paid to the owner. This principle appeared in all later preliminary and final drafts of American treaties.[38]

The best explanation of this change in American policy was that given by the American representatives in the attempt to negotiate a treaty with Portugal. They noted that the Armed Neutrality had produced great changes in the law concerning the number of goods defined as contraband, but now the designation of such goods was to be ended altogether in order to remove any temptation for the officers of belligerent ships to stop neutral vessels in the hope of profiting from the seizure of illegal merchandise. In the past the seizure of contraband moving by seas might have brought an enemy to its knees because of limited manufacturing resources, but that was no longer the case. Thus "the residue of the catalogue therefore are remains of a practice which continues after the causes producing it have ceased to exist; and it is become an abuse."[39] The Portuguese, who were unwilling to accept "free ships make free goods," did not agree with this reasoning, for they were obviously unwilling to accept an even greater departure from previous practice.[40] Nevertheless, the actions of the United States and this explanation of its reasoning indicated the American desire to break with the past, to mold the law of nations and their relations with other states into a framework that would more adequately reflect American needs and ideals.

Two proposals, to neutralize the "sugar islands" and

outlaw privateering, introduced by Benjamin Franklin at the Peace negotiations, are even more indicative of the American attitude. Franklin tried, in the first proposal, to remove a problem for neutral trade existing in every war, particularly those between Britain and France, but the idea had little chance for adoption in view of the economic interests of the states having colonies in the West Indies. Franklin's second proposal was also put forward in the unsuccessful attempts to negotiate treaties with Denmark, Portugal, and Great Britain and was finally adopted in the treaty with Prussia. In typically American terms, Franklin explained that there was ample reason for such a prohibition because:

> The practice of robbing merchants on the high seas, a remnant of the ancient piracy, though it may be accidently beneficial to particular persons, is far from being profitable to all engaged in it....Then there is the national loss of all the labor of so many men, during the time they have been employed robbing, who, besides, spend what they get in riot, drunkenness, debauchery, lose their habit of industry, are rarely fit for any sober business after a peace, and serve only to increase the number of highwaymen and housebreakers. Even the undertakers who have been fortunate are, by sudden wealth, led into expensive living, the habit of which continues when the means of supporting it cease, and finally ruins them. A just punishment for their having wantonly and unfeelingly ruined many honest, innocent traders and their families, whose substance was employed in serving the common interest of mankind.

The United States thus saw a means by which it could remove a threat to the morals of mankind, an action that it saw as self-denying because of the greater value of foreign ships that it could seize if privateering continued and the addition to its strength that a large corps of privateers would provide.[41]

American representatives also made two other proposals that, after being tried in several negotiations, were finally adopted in the Prussian treaty. The first placed definite limits on actions by belligerents against nonmilitary personnel and activities, reflecting the American desire to allow trade to continue in the midst of hostilities and provide for the welfare of mankind against the hazards of war.[42] The second dealt with prisoners of war and sought to improve their lot by preventing removal to tropical penal colonies and ending the need to negotiate, during hostilities, cartels or conventions for the welfare of prisoners.[43]

The treaty with Prussia that went into effect on 17 May 1786 was the most liberal of those negotiated by the United States and also the last to be undertaken before the ratification of the Consitution. Questions about the stability of the existing American government made substantive diplomatic exchanges difficult, if not impossible. Americans moved slowly toward a new form of central control. In view of this change, it is appropriate to make some observations about American policy up to 1789.

An analysis of American foreign policy and the law of nations reveals four major problems, each stemming from or contributing to an erroneous perception of both the law and the world of the eighteenth century. First, though it may not have been clear to all at the time, the French alliance combined with the absence of an Anglo-American commercial treaty effectively denied American commerce the protection of the law in the one case where such protection was vital—an Anglo-French war. Second, the American view of the law of nations as the international equivalent of domestic law was absurd because no sovereign authority existed, as it did domestically, to enforce the observance of the law if a nation decided that such compliance was not in its interest. Third, though genuinely drawn to the law of nations because the law of nature was the ultimate source of the necessary law, the United States aimed almost totally at establishing the stipulative law as the new source, particularly in regard to "free ships make free goods" and a limited definition of contraband. This is indicated by an examination of both its treaties and its support for the Armed Neutrality, which led Americans to believe, in the absence of any real challenge to that belief, that their policy had succeeded when, in fact, it had not. Finally, in turning to the law of nations the United States adopted a system that was fundamentally European in its origin and took for granted, in its operation, the balance of power, absolute monarchies, large standing armies, closed economic systems, and war as an instrument of national policy— the very principles that the United States, in the Revolution, had rejected. The United States thus adopted the forms of the law while ignoring its substance and placed its reliance on a system that, while it might serve its ideals and principles, could not safeguard its interests.

Why, in view of these flaws, did the United States adopt such a policy? American weakness, alienation from traditional forms of European diplomacy, need to expand commerce to promote economic prosperity, and limited perception of the law itself all made a policy based on the law of nations the only realistic choice that would unite interests and principles and produce a domestic consensus. Moreover, except perhaps for the French alliance and the absence of an Anglo-American treaty, the weaknesses of the policy were not particularly apparent to Americans of that day. In the eighteenth century, Americans, as they have throughout their history, had an almost infinite capacity to see themselves as right even in the face of evidence to the contrary. They believed that their commercial treaties and the Armed Neutrality had set down principles of the necessary law of nations. What had in fact been established, however, was an "American law of nations." When this "American law" was violated, as it was by Britain and France in the 1790s, the fault lay not in the treaties or the Armed Neutrality, but in the actions of the nations violating the law as perceived by the United States. Indeed, violations served to reinforce the American belief in the rightness of its position because such actions clearly stemmed from what Americans already knew: Europe was reactionary and corrupt.

The need was not the adoption of the European conception of the law of nations but rather greater efforts to gain the universal acceptance of the "American law" in order to fulfill the promise of the American Revolution.

The United States thus conceived of a world and a law that could not and did not exist in the eighteenth century. Americans saw themselves as the children of an enlightened age, but they existed in a world that was not very enlightened. They had, however, established the basis for an American foreign policy, the ideals and principles of which would last far into the future. It was a policy and a conception of the world perhaps best expressed by the American negotiators in regard to the inclusion of their principles into the Prussian treaty. They asked "why should not this law of nations go on improving: Ages have intervened between its several steps; but as knowledge of late increases rapidly, why should not these steps be quickened...?"[44]

## NOTES

1. Historians have moved away from Samuel Flagg Bemis's emphasis on political history in *The Diplomacy of the American Revolution* (rev. ed., Bloomington: Indiana Univ. Press, 1961) which, though it remains a seminal work, tends to describe rather than explain, and presents conclusions that, in light of more recent scholarship, seem simplistic. This tendency is clear in such books as Lawrence S. Kaplan, *Colonies into Nation* (New York: Macmillan Co., 1972); Paul Varg, *Foreign Policies of the Founding Fathers* (East Lansing: Michigan State Univ. Press, 1963); and Felix Gilbert, *To the Farewell Address* (Princeton: Princeton Univ. Press, 1961). The first two cover some of the same ground as Bemis, albeit in less detail, and point out that the American sense of uniqueness and distrust of the Old World were major forces in American policy. Gilbert takes an intellectual approach, examining the European influence on American policy although to some degree, particularly in the case of the philosophes, he overemphasizes it. Other treatments of the period, such as William C. Stinchcombe, *The American Revolution and the French Alliance* (Syracuse: Syracuse Univ. Press, 1969) and Richard B. Morris, *The Peacemakers* (New York: Harper and Row Publishers, 1965) continue these lines of investigation.

2. Emerich de Vattel, *The Law of Nations or the Principles of Natural Law Applied to the Conduct of the Affairs of Nations and Soveriegns,* trans. Charles L. Fenwick, *The Classics of International Law,* ed. James Brown Scott (Washington, D.C.: Carnegie Institution, 1916) Introduction, Sec. 18.

3. Plan of Treaties, 18 July 1776, Worthington Ford and others, eds., *Journals of the Continental Congress* (34 vols., Washington, D.C.: GPO, 1904-1937), V, 576-89.

4. Articles XXVI and XXVII, ibid., 585-86.

5. Treaty between Great Britain and the United Provinces, 1 December 1674, Articles I, II, III, IV, and VIII, Charles Jenkinson, 1st Earl of Liverpool, *A Collection of Treaties of Peace, Commerce, and Alliance Between Great Britain and other Powers, From the Year 1619 to 1734, To Which is Added A Discourse on the Conduct of the Government of Great Britain by C. Jenkinson Secretary of State* (London: 1781), pp. 50-52, 54-55. An added impetus is given to a comparison of the two documents because it was the provisions of the Anglo-Dutch Treaty of 1674 that served to provoke the Rule of 1756. The United States, in its treaty plan, was following a policy that would ultimately bring it into direct conflict with that rule.

6. Lyman Butterfield and others, eds., *Diary and Autobiography of John Adams* (4 vols., Cambridge, Massachusetts: Belknap Press,

1962), III, 315, 327-29. A question exists in respect to this statement and others made throughout the period as to what was meant by the term alliance. Felix Gilbert in *To the Farewell Address*, pp. 45-48, states that the founding fathers saw no difference between different types of alliances. Such an interpretation is questionable for, while the general term alliance was used to describe all types of treaty connections, in practice a sharp distinction was made between a commercial treaty, which was not entangling, and a treaty promising direct aid in time of war, which was. Thus Americans, with their strong desire to provide for future neutrality, noninvolvement in European affairs, and prosperity through increased trade, in speaking of an alliance were referring to a commercial treaty which they believed would provide the other party with enough commercial benefits to cancel out the need for a military treaty.

7. Butterfield and others, eds., *Diary and Autobiography of John Adams*, II, 236, III, 337-38; John Adams to John M. Jackson, December 30, 1817, Charles Francis Adams, ed., *The Works of John Adams* (10 vols., Boston: Little, Brown and Co., 1850-1856), X, 269-70; John Adams to Zebediah Adams, 21 June 1776; John Adams to John Winthrop, 23 June 1776; Edmund C. Burnett, ed., *Letters of Members of the Continental Congress* (8 vols., Washington, D.C.: Carnegie Institution, 1921-1936), I, 501, 502.

8. For the origin and operation of the Rule of 1756, see Richard Pares, *Colonial Blockade and Neutral Rights, 1739-1763* (Oxford: Clarendon Press, 1938), pp. 180-84, 186-87, 194-95, 201, 224.

9. Article 12 of the Treaty of Commerce between Great Britain and Russia, 2 December 1734 in the handwriting of Edward Randolph, 14 August 1781, Ford and others, eds., *Journals of the Continental Congress*, XXI, 863. This article was used as a basis to define contraband in an Ordinance Ascertaining What Captures on Water Shall be Legal, finally adopted on 4 December 1781. Traite de Commerce entre la Grand-Bretagne et la Russe, 20 June 1766, Article XI, George Frederick de Martens, *Recueil de Traites* (Paris: 1814), I, 395-96.

10. Treaty of Amity and Commerce [France], 6 February 1778, Articles XI, XII, XVI, XXV, XXVI, and XXXI, Treaty of Alliance [France], 6 February 1778, Articles XI and XII, David Hunter Miller, ed., *Treaties and Other International Acts of the United States of America* (8 vols., Washington, D.C.: GPO, 1931-1948), II, 10-11, 14-15, 20-23, 26, 39-40.

11. Andrew Adams to Oliver Wolcott, 22 July 1778; Samuel Adams to Peter Thacher, 11 August 1778; William Whipple to Josiah Bartlett, 27 July 1779; Burnett, ed., *Letters of Members*, III, 307-08, 347, IV, 345-46; John Adams to Samuel Adams, 28 July 1778; John Adams to James Warren, 4 August 1778; John Adams to Roger Sherman, 6

December 1778; Francis Wharton, ed., *The Revolutionary Diplomatic Correspondence of the United States* (6 vols., Washington, D.C.: GPO, 1889), II, 667-68, 675-77, 852.

12. Instructions to John Adams, 8 August 1781, Ford and others, eds., *Journals of the Continental Congress,* XXI, 876-80.

13. Instructions to the Agents in Europe on the Plan of Treaties, 24 September 1776, Ford and others, eds., *Journals of the Continental Congress,* V, 813-17.

14. Harrison and others, Committee of Foreign Affairs to the Commissioners at Paris, 18 October 1777; Wharton, ed., *Revolutionary Diplomatic Correspondence,* II, 412-13.

15. Benjamin Franklin to M. Grand, 17 October 1778, ibid., 784-85; Proclamation to Privateers, 9 May 1778; Ford and others, eds., *Journals of the Continental Congress,* XI, 486.

16. Benjamin Franklin to Count Vergennes, 18 June 1780; Wharton, ed., *Revolutionary Diplomatic Correspondence,* III, 801-03.

17. John Adams to the President of Congress, 10 April 1780, ibid., 606-08.

18. Traite de Commerce entre la Grand-Bretagne et la Russe, 20 June 1766, Article XI, George Frederick de Martens, *Recueil de Traites,* I, 395-96.

19. Treaty of Amity and Commerce [Netherlands], 8 October 1782, Article XXIV, Miller, ed., *Treaties and Other International Acts,* II, 79-80.

20. Committee of Foreign Affairs to the Agents in Europe, 5 October 1780, Wharton, ed., *Revolutionary Diplomatic Correspondence,* IV, 80-81; Report of the Admiralty Board, 21 October 1780, 3 November 1780, agreed to by Congress on 27 November 1780, Ford and others, eds., *Journals of the Continental Congress,* XVIII, 1008, 1097-98.

21. Ordinance Ascertaining what Captures on Water shall be Legal, 4 December 1781, Ford and others, eds., *Journals of the Continental Congress,* XXI, 1153-58. For the evolution of this ordinance, see 14 August 1781, 861-68, and 14 September 1781, 961-65.

22. The best treatment of Catherine's motives appears in Isabel de Madariaga, *Britain, Russia, and the Armed Neutrality* (New Haven: Yale Univ. Press, 1962). For an examination of the problems resulting from the American misconception of the real reasons for the declaration, see David M. Griffiths, "American Commercial Diplomacy in Russia," *William and Mary Quarterly,* Ser. 3, 37 (1970), 379-410; which deals with the ill-fated Dana mission. For an earlier study of the American attitude toward the League, see William S. Carpenter, "The United States and the League of Neutrals of 1780," *American Journal of International Law,* 15 (1921), 511-22.

23. John Adams to the President of Congress, 26 April 1780, Wharton, ed., *Revolutionary Diplomatic Correspondence,* III, 632-33;

Benjamin Franklin to Robert Morris, 3 June 1780, John Bigelow, ed., *The Works of Benjamin Franklin,* Federal Edition (12 vols., New York: G. P. Putnam's Sons, 1904), VIII, 339-40; Samuel Huntington to Reverend James Cogswell, 22 July 1780, Burnett, ed., *Letters of Members,* VIII, 285; James Madison to Edmund Pendleton, 7 November 1780, William T. Hutchinson and William R. E. Rashal, eds., *Papers of James Madison* (9 vols., Chicago: Univ. of Chicago Press, 1961-), II, 165-68.

24. John Adams to Digges, 13 May 1780, John Adams to the President of Congress, 20 May 1780, Wharton, ed., *Revolutionary Diplomatic Correspondence,* III, 676-77, 693-96.

25. John Adams to the President of Congress, 14 April 1780, ibid., 612-14.

26. Benjamin Franklin to Robert Morris, 3 June 1780, Bigelow, ed., *Works of Benjamin Franklin,* VIII, 339-40.

27. Thomas Jefferson to Burrill Carnes, 22 September 1787, Julian P. Boyd, ed., *The Papers of Thomas Jefferson* (18 vols., Princeton: Princeton Univ. Press, 1950-), XII, 164-65.

28. Instructions to Mr. Jay, 6 May 1794, U.S., *American State Papers, Foreign Relations* (Washington, D.C.: Gales and Seaton, 1832), I, 472-74.

29. Report of the Committeee Concerning the Armed Neutrality, 5 October 1780, Ford and others, eds., *Journals of the Continental Congress,* XVIII, 905-06.

30. John Adams: Memorial to the States General, 8 March 1781, Wharton, ed., *Revolutionary Diplomatic Correspondence,* IV, 274-75.

31. Report on American Participation in a European Neutral Confederation, 12 June 1783, Ford and others, eds., *Journals of the Continental Congress,* XXVI, 392-94. See also Proceedings of Congress as to the Russian Mission, 21 May 1783, 348-54, 22 May 1783, 354-57.

32. Instructions for Negotiating Treaties of Amity and Commerce, 29 October 1783, Ford and others, eds., *Journals of the Continental Congress,* XXV, 753-57; Report of the Secretary for Foreign Affairs on M. Dumas's Letter of 20 March 1783, 3 June 1783, Wharton, ed., *Revolutionary Diplomatic Correspondence,* VI, 473-74.

33. From the Commissioners to the Marquis of Carmarthen, 4 April 1786, *Diplomatic Correspondence of the United States from the Signing of the Definitive Treaty of Peace, 10th September, 1783, to the Adoption of the Constitution, March 4, 1789* (3 vols., Washington, D.C.: Blair and Ives, 1837), II, 602-04.

34. Plan of Treaties, 18 July 1776, Articles XXVI and XXVII, Plan of a Treaty of Commerce [Netherlands], 22 February 1779, Articles XIX and XXVIII, Plan of a Treaty of Amity and Commerce [Sweden], 28 September 1782, Articles IX and XV, Ford and others, eds., *Journals of*

*the Continental Congress*, V, 585-86, XIII, 228, 231, XXIII, 616, 618-19; Treaty of Amity and Commerce [France], 6 February 1778, Articles XVI and XXV, Treaty of Amity and Commerce [Netherlands], 8 October 1782, Articles X and XII, Treaty of Amity and Commerce [Sweden], 3 April 1783, Articles VII and XIV, Miller, ed., *Treaties and Other International Acts*, II, 14-15, 16-17, 68, 70-71, 128-29, 141-42.

35. Report on Letters from the American Ministers in Europe, Provisions to be called for in Treaties, 20 December 1783, Provision 6, Boyd, ed., *The Papers of Thomas Jefferson*, VI, 395.

36. Draught of a Treaty of Amity and Commerce [Denmark], 15 September 1784, Article XII, De Thulemier to the American Commissioners, 24 January 1785, Draught of a Treaty of Amity and Commerce [Portugal], March-April 1786, Article XII, Boyd, ed., *The Papers of Thomas Jefferson*, VII, 482-83, 626, IX, 415; Project of a Treaty of Amity and Commerce [Prussia], Submitted by Baron Thulemier, 10 April 1784, Articles IX and XVI, Counter Project of a Treaty of Amity and Commerce [Prussia], 8 October 1784, Article XII, Answer to the Observations on the Provisional Treaty with Prussia Submitted by Baron De Thulemier, 17 March 1785, Draft of a Treaty of Amity and Commerce, 11 October 1785, Article V, Draft of a Treaty of Amity and Commerce [Great Britain], 29 July 1785, Article XII, *Diplomatic Correspondence, 1783-1789*, I, 446-47, 449, 523, 554-60, 667, II, 411; A Treaty of Amity and Commerce [Prussia], 10 September 1785, Article XII, Miller, ed., *Treaties and Other International Acts*, II, 170-71.

37. Plan of Treaties, 18 July 1776, Article XXVII, Plan of a Treaty of Commerce [Netherlands], 22 February 1779, Article XXIX, Plan of a Treaty of Amity and Commerce [Sweden], 28 September 1782, Article XVI, Ford and others, eds., *Journals of the Continental Congress*, V, 585-86, XIII, 232, XXIII, 619-20; Treaty of Amity and Commerce [France], 6 February 1778, Article XXVI, Treaty of Amity and Commerce [Netherlands], 8 October 1782, Article XXIV, Treaty of Amity and Commerce [Sweden], 3 April 1783, Articles VIII, IX, and X, Miller, ed., *Treaties and Other International Acts*, II, 21-22, 79-80, 129-31. See also Project of a Treaty of Amity and Commerce [Prussia], Submitted by Baron Thulemier, 10 April 1784, Articles XI and XII, *Diplomatic Correspondence, 1783-1789*, I, 447-48.

38. Report on Letters from the American Ministers in Europe, Provisions to be called for in Treaties, 20 December 1783, Provision 5, Draught of a Treaty of Amity and Commerce [Denmark], 15 September 1784, Article XIII, Draught of a Treaty of Amity and Commerce [Portugal], March-April 1786, Article XIII, Boyd, ed., *The Papers of Thomas Jefferson*, VI, 394-95, VII, 483, IX, 415-16; Counter Project of a Treaty of Amity and Commerce [Prussia], 8 October 1784, Article XIII, Draft of a Treaty of Amity and Commerce [Great Britain], 29 July 1785, Article XIII, *Diplomatic Correspondence, 1783-1789*, I,

523-24; II, 411-12; Treaty of Amity and Commerce [Prussia], 10 September 1785, Article XIII, Miller, ed., *Treaties and Other International Acts,* II, 171-72.

39. Observations by the American Commissioners, March-April 1786, Boyd, ed., *The Papers of Thomas Jefferson,* IX, 426-31.

40. Observations by the Portuguese Minister, March-April 1786, Additional Observations by the Portuguese Minister, March-April 1786, ibid., 424-26, 432-33.

41. Benjamin Franklin to Richard Oswald, 14 January 1783, Wharton, ed., *Revolutionary Diplomatic Correspondence,* VI, 210-11; Draught of a Treaty of Amity and Commerce [Denmark], 15 September 1784, Article XXIII, Draught of a Treaty of Amity and Commerce [Portugal], March-April 1786, Article XXIII, Boyd, ed., *The Papers of Thomas Jefferson,* VII, 486, IX, 419; Reasons in Support of the New Proposed Articles in the Treaties of Commerce, 10 November 1784, From the Commissioners to Baron De Thulemier, 10 November 1784, Draft of a Treaty of Amity and Commerce [Great Britain], 29 July 1785, Article XXIII, *Diplomatic Correspondence, 1783-1789,* I, 531-32, 532-34, II, 415; Treaty of Amity and Commerce [Prussia], 10 September 1785, Article XXIII, Miller, ed., *Treaties and Other International Acts,* II, 178-79.

42. Instructions to the Commissioners for Negotiating Treaties of Amity and Commerce, 7 May 1784, Boyd, ed., *The Papers of Thomas Jefferson,* VII, 266-69. The provisions dealing with civilians appear in the same articles as do those outlawing privateers: therefore see note 39 for the relevant citations.

43. Draught of a Treaty of Amity and Commerce [Denmark], 15 September 1784, Article XXIV, Draught of a Treaty of Amity and Commerce [Portugal], March-April 1786, Article XXIV, Boyd, ed., *The Papers of Thomas Jefferson,* VII, 486-87, IX, 419-20; Draft of a Treaty of Amity and Commerce [Great Britain], 29 July 1785, Article XXIV, *Diplomatic Correspondence, 1783-1789,* II, 415-16; A Treaty of Amity and Commerce [Prussia], 10 September 1785, Article XXIV, Miller, ed., *Treaties and Other International Acts,* II, 179-81.

44. Reasons in Support of the New Proposed Articles in the Treaties of Commerce, 10 March 1784, *Diplomatic Correspondence, 1783-1789,* I, 532-34.

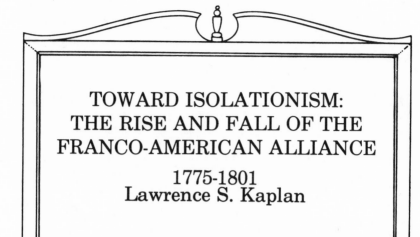

# TOWARD ISOLATIONISM: THE RISE AND FALL OF THE FRANCO-AMERICAN ALLIANCE

## 1775-1801
## Lawrence S. Kaplan

Isolationism has always held an elusive quality for American diplomatic historians. The term itself is no older than the 1920s, and fittingly is identified with a revulsion against the entanglements of world war.[1] This rejection of Europe was undergirded by an earlier religious image of a New World arising out of the failure of the Old, sitting apart on its transatlantic hill. These Calvinist expectations of a New Jerusalem in turn received reinforcement from the secular thought of the Enlightenment, which contrasted the simple, egalitarian, free society of eighteenth-century America with the complex, class-ridden, war-plagued societies of Europe. As a consequence of this bifurcated vision of the world Washington's Farewell Address of 1796 became an enduring symbol of America's isolation. His message was directed against the French alliance of 1778, the first and only entangling political commitment to Europe the United States made until the framing of the North Atlantic Treaty in 1949.

An earlier version of this paper was presented in a colloquium at the Woodrow Wilson International Center for Scholars, Washington, D.C., on 24 July 1974. A portion of the essay appeared in *Historical Reflections/Reflexions Historiques,* 3 (Summer 1976), 69-81.

For all but a few ideologues tied either to the mother country or to the wilderness, isolationism meant a freedom to enjoy access to all ports interested in receiving American products. It meant further a freedom from subservience to any foreign power, of the kind which had forced them into the service of a maternal economy or of dynastic wars in the past. Finally, it extended to a self-image of virtue and innocence that would be protected by advancing principles of peaceful relationships among nations.

The alliance with France violated these conceptions of America's position in the world. Conceivably, the potential contradiction between the profession of isolationism and the making of alliance lies in confusion over the meaning of "alliance." It may be resolved, according to Felix Gilbert, by accepting an eighteenth-century understanding of alliances which embrace both commercial agreements and military obligations.[2] There were no genuine distinctions between a treaty of commerce and a treaty of alliance. So when the Founding Fathers spoke of a foreign alliance as a desideratum, they could reconcile their wish for a commercial connection with refusal of political bonds. There is evidence enough in the language used by policymakers during the life of the twenty-three year alliance to buttress this thesis. Both the French and Americans intertwined the provisions of the treaty of amity and commerce with the claims of the treaty of alliance in the 1790s. And the model treaty of 1776 lumped political and commercial considerations together.

But there is also abundant evidence that the men who framed foreign policy during the Revolution recognized clearly the distinctions between the two kinds of treaties. They wanted France to be obligated in the Model Treaty without cost to themselves. They failed to entice the French under these terms, and they knew they failed. If they accepted political and military entanglement it was because they felt they had no choice. The most they could do would be to limit the potential damage subservience to

France's national interest would have. None of the framers was surprised to find France willing to limit American territorial claims in peace negotiations in 1782, or to keep West Indian ports closed to American ships in the 1790s, or even to make the United States, if possible, an equivalent of the Cisalpine Republic. Napoleon Bonaparte was not only the end product of France's revolution in this period, but the logical extension of fears they had always entertained of foreign control.

That a successful defiance of England would require the help of Europe was understood even before separation was made official. The Continental Congress established a five-man Committee of Secret Correspondence on 19 November 1775, "for the sole purpose of corresponding with our friends in Great Britain, Ireland, and other parts of the world."[3] Since the voices of America's friends in and out of Parliament had either been stilled or had turned away from the colonies, the "other parts of the world" became an immediate object of attention. The most notable part was France, England's familiar enemy, which had been periodically testing colonial discontent for ten years to see how it might be turned to its own advantage.

The French Court's interest was not ephemeral. Vergennes, the foreign minister, welcomed the dispatch of Silas Deane, a former delegate to the Congress from Connecticut and merchant connected with Robert Morris's firm in Philadelphia. It was not coincidental that Morris was a member of the committee which presented the Model Treaty of 1776. Deane was joined by Arthur Lee, the committee's agent in London and colonial agent from Massachusetts. He was the brother of Richard Henry Lee, another member of the Committee of Secret Correspondence. The scene was set then both for the supply of munitions, weapons, and equipment to the colonies by indirect means from the French and Spanish Crowns which permitted a vital and massive infusion of energy to the colonial war effort and an opportunity for fiscal confusion and personal profit for the American agents involved in the transactions. In all these dealings the substance was commerce, not politics; trade, not military obligations.

The function France was performing should have fitted perfectly the message of Thomas Paine in his *Common Sense,* when he expressed a few months later that "the true interest of America is to steer clear of Europe's contentions, which she never can do while, by her dependence on Britain, she is made the makeweight in the scale of British politics." More than this, he asserted that "Our plan is commerce, and that, well attended to, will secure us the peace and friendship of Europe." It also reflected the thinking of John Adams who had been the prime mover in the summer of 1776 in drawing up a model treaty. His Plan of 1776 operated on the assumption that Europe would sue for America's trade and would promote America's independence to secure this advantage as well as to weaken British colonial power. France was the vital cog in the plan that would serve the war effort but without the price of entangling reciprocal obligations. Adams's language could not be plainer: "I am not for soliciting any political connection, or military assistance, or indeed, naval from France. I wish for nothing but commerce, a mere marine treaty with them."[4]

As a consequence of a confidence bordering on truculence the American treaty plan of 1776 elaborated on liberal ideas of international law and freedom of the seas, ideas appealing to the philosophers of France and to the naval competitors of the great seapower of the day. More controversial in tone was the self-denial Article 9 would impose on the French, forcing the king to promise that "he shall never invade, nor, under any pretense, attempt to possess himself of any of the territories of the mainland which had been French or Spanish in the past.[5] Almost grudgingly it seemed, the French would be permitted to keep whatever West Indian possessions they acquired by virtue of joining the Americans.

137

Such euphoria as this plan reflected dissipated rapidly in 1776. The war went badly for American arms and American morale. While the surreptitious aid given by the French and Spanish was substantial, it did not produce the desired effects on the war effort. As a result, the demands on France moved from commercial support to military assistance to a promise of reciprocal political and military obligation, in return for open adherence to the war. It was the Americans, and not the French, who became the suitor for an alliance. An increasingly nervous awareness that the world was not so well ordered as the Paine scenario had implied informed the advice given the ministers in France by the Committee of Secret Correspondence and its successor, the Committee of Foreign Affairs. Deane and Lee, joined by Franklin late in 1776, were permitted to relax the requirements for French aid. They were to assure the French of no future allegiance to Britain, of no trade advantages to any other power greater than to the French benefactor, and an additional agreement to make no termination of war, should the French enter it, without full notice to the French partner.[6]

As American confidence in its own power weakened, the commissioners' importunities became more frantic. The American distress abroad was compounded by the rivalry between Arthur Lee and his family on the one side, with Silas Deane, supported by Franklin, on the other. While this controversy ultimately became a major cause célèbre in the Continental Congress, ruining both Deane's and Lee's careers, it is worth noting that their position on the French alliance differed in no significant way before the treaty was made. Both men were willing to offer promises along with vague threats to move the French from their cautious stance. Deane warned the French that without sufficient help the Americans would be forced to reunite with the British. An independent America, on the other hand, would make France a successor to Britain in the domination of world commerce.[7] Arthur Lee pursued a different tactic when he appealed to the French to witness America standing up to Britain and serving them by striking out at Britain's pretensions. "We are left like Hercules in his cradle, to strangle the serpent that annoys all Europe."[8]

The French foreign office listened and bided its time. Port officials returned British prizes Americans brought too openly into French cities. There was no acknowledgement of the declaration of American independence, even as supplies and soldiers found their way to America from France. It required the victory at Saratoga in the fall of 1777, and more important, signs of British accommodation to America's early war aims before France was willing to make an alliance formally and accept the price of war for its pains. And when the treaty was finally concluded, the brave words of Adams and Paine were forgotten. Not only did the United States reassure the French about the termination of the war and about commercial benefits, but a specific entanglement was made in Article 11, which was not to be found in the Model Treaty, in the form of mutual guarantees "from the present time and forever, to wit, the united states to his most Christian Majesty the present Possessions of the Crown of France in America as well as those which it may acquire by the future Treaty of peace...."[9] Thus the commissioners made an agreement which bound the United States for an indefinite future to the defense of a foreign power's territory in America, a sure guarantee of involvement in the European balance of power in any subsequent quarrel between Britain and France.

The American response was one of relief and gratitude. The Congress considered the treaty officially on 4 May 1778, and ratified it two days later with little commentary beyond directing the commissioners "to present the grateful acknowledgements of this Congress to his most Christian majesty for his truly magnanimous conduct respecting these States in the said generous and disinterested treaties."[10] The only question raised by the commissioners concerned the mutual prohibitions of duties on exports between the United States and the French West Indies. These articles were removed.

The appreciation was genuine and appropriate. France's decision for alliance was a decision for war with Britain, and it confirmed American independence, if not victory on the battlefield. Given the turmoil of the Congress, the divisions within the new nation, and the uncertainties of the military results, France gave the United States a remarkable gift—that of a successful conclusion to the Revolution. It agreed to renounce its concerns with former colonies in the New World, and to maintain "effectually the liberty, Sovereignty, and independance absolute and unlimited of the said United States, as well in Matters of gouvernement as in commerce."[11] In the short run the benefits outweighed any debits.

Generous as the French were, their interest in the success of the United States was always subordinated to their greater interests in their financial status, maintenance of the monarchical principle, and cultivation of their more important alliance with Spain. If America could achieve its objectives in war without clashing with France's other concerns, the French ally would gladly be of service, as long as the paternal guidance of His Most Christian Majesty would govern American behavior. But when it became apparent first to the new peace commission abroad—John Adams, John Jay, and Benjamin Franklin—and then to the Congress that France was prepared to accept less than the borders the United States wanted or the fisheries New England demanded, the relationship soon became uneasy. From the French side came charges of ingratitude as Minister Gerard was caught up on the side of Deane in the Lee-Deane dispute, and as his successor had to pursue French interests by influencing public opinion through the subsidized journalism of Thomas Paine and Hugh Henry Brackenridge.

American restiveness was more openly expressed. A

generalized anti-Gallican and anti-Catholic sentiment had its center in New England, but its vibrations were felt throughout the states. Friends of France like Jefferson were sorely disappointed over the quality of French military assistance. Distrust over the purposes of French aid was widespread from the beginnings of the alliance, as secret negotiations among the European powers between 1778 and 1782 evoked suspicions first of French disinterest in America's transappalachian ambitions, and then of the ally's collaboration with the British and Spanish in an attempt to confine the United States to the Atlantic littoral. These suspicions were justified, and most of the French *arrières pensées* about America were exposed before the war ended. Even more open were the pressures exerted by French officials in America to bend Congress's policies to France's wishes. Luzerne, in the best manner of a patron chiding a client for his errors, made Congress revise its instruction to the American commission abroad from a general statement that the commission be guided by "the advice and opinion of the French peace negotiators" to a more specific mandate that it "undertake nothing in the negotiations for peace or truce without their knowledge and concurrence."[12] Since the Court disliked John Adams, his appointment was broadened to include first two and then four commissioners.

But ironically as the war drew to a close, the Congress became more compliant rather than more resistant to French designs. The explanation for docility was not in the venality of politicians on the payroll, even though that roll was long, illustrious and well padded. It lies more in the increasing awareness of the fragility of the Confederation and in the psychological and financial drain of the long war with Britain. To men such as Robert R. Livingston, the first secretary for foreign affairs of the Confederation, and Robert Morris, its superintendent of finances from 1781 to 1783, there was no substitute for French support in this period.

Morris, in his critical capacity as finance minister, reveals this dependence clearly. Buoyed by the Franco-American victory at Yorktown, he expressed his surprise to Franklin in December 1781, that the United States made so many purchases in Holland. "If everything else were equal the generous conduct of France towards us has been such that I cannot but think every possible preference ought to be given to the manufacturers of that nation."[13] Whether this sentiment reflected the state of his personal investments more than the national is less material than the importance he gave to the continuing French financial support. At the same time he recognized the price of this support. A few months later, after Congress heeded his advice, he had second thoughts about the relationship and urged merchants to draw upon Spanish and Dutch creditors rather than on Frenchmen exclusively. In July 1782, he lamented that France had not granted all aid as loan rather than a gift because "I do not think the weight of the debt would be so great as the weight of an obligation is generally found to be." No matter how assiduously Morris may have been pursuing his private welfare, he understood the public's as well.[14]

As for Livingston, he was alarmed at the freewheeling behavior of the commissioners who wandered over Europe denouncing the ally, dickering with the enemy, and ignoring the will of the Congress. Jay, prodded by Adams, had exposed a secret French memorandum which presumably would have ended the war, with the British and Spanish sharing territory between the mountains and the Mississippi; while Franklin concluded a separate agreement with the British which left the French no alternative but to accept. Jay's letter chafing at Congressional fetters discomfited Livingston. Jay insisted on the Americans accepting British terms if they were appropriate: "we are under no obligation to persist in the war to gratify this court. But can it be wise to instruct your commissioners to speak only as the French minister shall give them utterance."[15]

Livingston was not alone in his nervousness. He represented the sense of the Congress preoccupied with financial cares and with the impediments to governance. While Hamilton could admit that it was "not improbably that it had been the policy of France to procrastinate the definite acknowledgemt. of our Independence...in order to keep us more knit to herself & untill her own interests could be negotiated," he preferred to compare French benevolence with British malevolence.[16] Jay and his colleagues had erred in not showing preliminary articles to the ally before signing and in working out a separate and secret article on Florida boundaries with the British. There was a churlishness implicit in the commissioners' behavior. On balance, as Madison suggested, the total role of France deserves gratitude, not reproach.

Congressional reaction was not simply shock over the improprieties of their representatives abroad. It represented as well fear over French displeasure. John Mercer of Virginia was particularly exercised over the Florida issue, for fear that an angry France would turn around and join Britain in a punitive attack on the United States. Jay's indiscretions played into British hands by creating divisions between the allies, from which only the British could profit. The secret Florida article, enlarging that territory if it fell back into British hands, may have been deliberately contrived by Britain "not for the sake of the territory ceded to her, but as a means of disuniting the U.S. & France, as inconsistent with the spirit of the Alliance."[17] As for France's retribution, Luzerne remonstrated with Livingston and congressmen about the behavior of the Commissioners. The king "did not think he has such allies to deal with." In answer to a question about France's intention to lodge an official complaint to the Congress, "M. Marbois [France's chargé d'affaires] answered that Great Powers never *complained* but that they *felt* and *remembered*."[18] And this ominous note emerged before the knowledge of the secret article had reached the French. As for a congressional rebuke to the envoys, the Congress consoled itself that the ministers did not literally break the treaty and that France was not directly involved in the Florida border problem. So while the commissioners were reprimanded for ignoring congressional instructions, it was done in such a way that their sensibilities would not be ruffled and that the "perfect harmony and confidence" of the ally would be maintained.[19]

Embarrassed as Congress was over this issue, it is questionable if its fears were essentially military or political in nature. The American delegates were neither as naive nor as dependent as the French had hoped. Their problem was fiscal, and the one response they feared most was the rupture of the pipeline of credits and supplies from France to the American economy. Morris raised the question in January 1783, when he informed Congress of a multi-million livre gap between American commitments and American credits, and asked if he should take the risk of France refusing to honor bills. Congress decided to move on the assumption that even if peace came quickly, "France would prefer an advance in our favor to exposing us to the necessity of resorting to G.B. for it; and that if the war sd. continue the necessity of such an aid to its prosecution would continue."[20] In short, Congress displayed much the same kind of *Realpolitik* Franklin showed to Vergennes when the latter had upbraided the American diplomat for faithlessness to the alliance. Franklin replied by asking for more funds from the French to repair the damaged ties. The major difference was that Americans at home found it less politic to rub French sensibilities quite as raw as Americans abroad were prepared to do. Ultimately a committee was appointed to consider application for more loans on the grounds that the monies used for the army's disbanding would leave a sense of gratitude to the French among ex-soldiers. The alternative, as the French were subtly reminded, was internal convulsions among unpaid veterans which would not serve France's interests.[21] So much for American subservience to the claims of the alliance.

The treaty lost much of its significance to both parties after the war ended.[22] France had too many other problems plaguing its society in the 1780s to place any priority on its American investment. With few immediate benefits on the horizon, subsidies to American journalists were no longer necessary, even if they could have been afforded. France's complaisance over America's inability to repay its debts reflects the comfort the government was able to take in a weak and divided nation that had only France to turn to for support, no matter how attenuated the relationship should become.

Actually, France and things French prospered enormously during the Confederation. Appreciation for the French role in the Revolution took the form of a rise in interest in the French language and culture. Whatever the political differences and dynastic ambitions of the Crown, France had proven itself a friend, and French friends of America wanted America to succeed as a model for the less favored parts of the world. The lionizing experiences of Franklin and Jefferson in France, and the influence they had on the budding French revolutionaries were flattering to all Americans. In this light the alliance was a symbol of a sentimental bond, rather than a contractual obligation. The duties of treaties, even the fulfillment of trade concessions, were of less moment than the adulation of Lafayette, Brissot, or Chastellux. It was even possible for Frenchmen less worshipful of Americans to wish the United States well, even as they wished them weak and dependent upon France's favor.

What Jefferson, in particular, had wanted from France was a commercial relationship with political overtones. Concessions in admission of American tobacco and whale oil would advance not only the interest of Virginia planters and New England fishermen, but would also shift the American commerce from British to French channels. As minister to France and later as secretary of

145

state, Jefferson regarded France as a counterweight to
the dangerous irredentist British power, political and
economic. In failing to achieve these objectives, he
recognized that political instability and fiscal ineptitude
more than political hostility accounted for the frustra-
tions he met.

But even as he sought French assistance, Jefferson
recognized the dangers of entanglement. France's failure,
after the Revolution, to liberalize American commerce
with the West Indies or its earlier unwillingness, as
guarantor of the Peace of Paris, to help Americans push
the British out of Northwest posts or to defend American
shipping in the Mediterranean against Barbary pirates
might have evoked stronger reactions from Americans. If
they did not, a subliminal recognition of a counterpart
guarantee to French possessions may have checked their
anger. There was an underlying uneasiness over the
French relationship experienced by American leaders of
every persuasion. They agreed that the weakness of the
Confederation required drastic remedies to cope with a
hostile world. Madison and Jefferson, as well as Jay and
Morris, believed that France as well as Spain and Britain
was part of that world. For James Monroe the quarrel
between him and Jay over the abortive treaty with Spain
in 1786, which would have closed the Mississippi River to
American shipping, excluded France; for both men
France's role was that of Spain's patron. Similarly,
Jefferson could join with Jay in deploring Franklin's
consular agreement with France of 1782 for its apparent
grant of excessive privileges to French consuls in
America; they smacked of extraterritoriality.[23]

Although the alliance survived, it lacked vitality. When
its implications were considered, they frightened American statesmen. The language of the Constitutional
Convention and of the Federalist Papers tells the feelings
of the framers about entangling alliances, and it tells also
of the continuing consensus of future Jeffersonians and
Hamiltonians. Francophilism had no constituents in the

Convention at Philadelphia in 1787, as far as political ties were concerned. Within the Confederation the differences in foreign affairs had never been between proponents and antagonists of alliance; rather, they were between xenophobes hoping to remove all foreign connections and nationalists who wanted central power to manage those connections better. Monroe and Elbridge Gerry belonged to the former category in this period; their answer was to reduce a foreign establishment which would, in turn, minimize foreign relations. Gerry looked upon the French edict discriminating against American trade in the West Indies as symbolic of American impotence in international relations. The only solution for the United States was withdrawal.[24]

No such pessimism dominated the Convention and the defenders of the Constitution. While the Federalist Papers—particularly Jay's early contribution—hypothecated the consequences of the dissolution of the Confederation and the subsequent intervention of foreign powers, they also cited the Constitution as the instrument to dissuade hostile Europeans from intervening. Not the French alliance, but American internal power, will save the nation. If alliance was mentioned, it was pejoratively. Jay wrote in Federalist number Five that if the nation broke into rival units, it is likely that "each of them should be more desirous to guard against foreign dangers by foreign alliances, than to guard against foreign dangers by alliances between themselves....How many conquests did Romans and others make in the character of allies?" In number Four he had specifically identified France, along with Spain and Britain, as potential foreign allies to tempt rival American republics. There was no distinction here between present ally and late enemy.

The record of the first few years of the Federal Union in which Jefferson and Hamilton shared power in the Cabinet discloses no significant shift in sentiment over the French alliance. While Hamilton and his followers moved quickly toward an appreciation of a strong British commercial connection and thereby to a depreciation of the French treaties, Jefferson did not find the treaties of alliance or of amity and commerce equally important to him. It is not that he advocated the termination of the connections. The threat of British reconquest and commercial enslavement appeared stronger to him than before, and France's role as a weapon to break loose from Britain's economic control appealed to him and to Madison in the House of Representatives. Moreover, the early phases of the French Revolution inspired pride in American contribution to France's political enlightenment. But the sluggish response of presumably liberal France to the secretary of state's overtures revived all his suspicions and annoyances. Revolutionary France should have none of the old regime's excuses for failing to accommodate the economic needs of the United States. When the National Assembly imposed special duties on all foreign ships carrying commerce to France, Jefferson found this "such an act of hostility against our navigation, as was not to have been expected from the friendship of that nation."[25]

Many of these feelings receded when France and England went to war in 1793. France, now a republic, was challenged by British monarchism. And when Hamilton emerged openly as the powerful American champion of British interests, the role of France assumed a new character to the Jeffersonian. The alliance was pushed into the forefront of a Cabinet debate, by virtue of Hamilton's goading Washington into a proclamation of neutrality in the European war. The secretary of the treasury welcomed the Anglo-French crisis as an opportunity to break with France and realign American policy formally toward Britain. He could not have found a more sensitive issue with which to challenge his political opponents—Jefferson, Madison, Monroe and the Republican leaders of the North, George Clinton of New York, and Alexander Dallas of Pennsylvania. For neutrality was their object, as well as his, but it was an objective they did not wish to publicize in any way embarrassing to or injurious to the French war effort. Initially, they were willing to settle for a proclamation, provided that the word "neutrality" was excluded from the text.[26]

What they wished to avoid was the potential conflict between the obligations of the treaty of alliance, which could bring them into war in defense of the French West Indies, and American vulnerability to British economic and naval power, which would make war a disaster for the United States. Consequently, they spent their energies in the spring of 1793, where possible, on the more acceptable subject raised by Hamilton: namely, the illegitimacy of the French republic as an excuse for breaking the alliance and refusing to accept its envoy. As Jefferson indignantly wrote to Gouverneur Morris in Paris, "We surely cannot deny to any nation that right whereon our own government is founded, that every one may govern itself according to whatever form it pleases."[26] Madison, under the pen name of "Helvidius," asked his readers to "suppose" that conditions had been reversed—that American Congressmen had all been killed, that an interregnum resulted in which the states of South Carolina and Georgia were in danger of being overrun without the interposition of French arms. "Is it not manifest, that as the treaty is the treaty of the United States, not of their government, the people of the United States could not forfeit their right to the guaranty of their territory by the accidental suspension of their government; and that any attempt on the part of France, to evade the obligations of the treaty, by pleading the suspension of government, or by refusing to acknowledge it, would justly have been received with universal indignation, as an ignominious perfidy?"[28] More than illogic and ingratitude was involved. Monroe uncovered a Hamiltonian plot "to separate us from France & ultimately unite us with England."[29]

All of the above sentiments were echoed and reinforced

by the numerous democratic societies which sprang up throughout the country in 1793. Whether they were the heirs of the Sons of Liberty or spawns of the French Jacobin societies, they served to promote friendship with France and fidelity to the alliance.[30] Their primary note, and that of Jeffersonian leadership as well, was that France was fighting America's battle abroad. And America's service to the alliance would not be belligerency, but economic aid for which neutrality was a prerequisite. But it would be "a fair neutrality," in Jefferson's words, in which American vessels carried goods to France from the West Indies, unimpeded according to liberal understandings of neutral rights, with produce for France and profit for America. Jefferson admitted that it would still be "a disagreeable pill to our friend."[31]

The Jeffersonians deluded themselves in believing they could have both neutrality and the alliance. It is customary to blame the indiscretions of Genêt, the youthful French minister in 1793, for spoiling the delicate relationship between the two countries. But could the claims of the alliance, under the circumstances, have permitted the kind of neutrality Jefferson preferred? The British navy obviously had no intention of permitting what they called contraband goods to move from French colonial ports in American ships, even if it would stimulate resentment in the United States. The French would have permitted Americans to remain technically out of the war only because they saw other services the alliance could extract from the United States in the form of the transfer of supplies in American ships, the arming of privateers in American ports, and the staging of invasions in American territory. When these services were refused in the name of neutrality, the French then invoked the relationship of 1778. They were prepared to relieve the United States of the burden of defending West Indian islands only if the Americans would invoke and fulfill the articles of the treaty of commerce concerning freedom of the seas. For this occasion, France linked the

150

two treaties.

Hamilton realized the sham of the alliance sooner than Jefferson. The Republicans erred first in thinking the proclamation would have been harmless if Hamilton had not perverted it. And they were mistaken later in emphasizing the unconstitutional action of the executive in taking the action, as if this was the source of the difficulties with the French. The secretary of state's stand on Genêt's attempts to arm vessels in American ports exposed a position on the treaties that violated its spirit, if not its letter. Did Article 24 of the Treaty of Amity and Commerce imply that this privilege would be open to the French, since it was specifically denied to the enemies of both countries? Jefferson's negative answer appeared to be a mean-spirited literal interpretation of the treaty, worthy of the Hamiltonians.[32] The French construction was not unreasonable. But if compliance meant war with Britain, the Jeffersonians preferred embarrassment with France.

This does not mean that Madison, who led the Republicans from the Congress after Jefferson retired from the Cabinet in 1793, would have taken the next step of a treaty with the British, which outraged France's sensibilities even further. Whether Jay's Treaty was the work of Hamilton's prudence or guile, it was a logical extension of the American neutrality in the war and of America's dependence upon British trade channels. While the terms stipulated that nothing in the document would affect obligations already binding on the signatory powers, the contents made a mockery of the Franco-American treaties. Article 24, forbidding foreign privateers from arming their ships in American ports, did not grant to the British what had been denied to the French in 1793; but it explicitly denied this privilege to the "ally." At the same time, the treaty gave Britain exactly the same concession that France had enjoyed since 1778 in bringing prizes captured from France into this country, directly in conflict with the French treaty. Combined with

151

the failure to challenge Britain's interpretation of neutral rights and Britain's inclusion of provisions as contraband, it was hardly surprising that France read betrayal of the alliance into Jay's Treaty.

France was right. Its anti-American measures, in the face of the American position, were not inordinate. Abandoned by the United States in the one area the Americans could help the French, the mistreatment of American vessels that followed Jay's Treaty in French waters, and the undeclared war against the new undeclared ally of Britain, could be considered fitting retribution. Certainly, some of the Jeffersonian reaction followed this line. Unhappy though they were with France's descending to Britain's level in depredations against American commerce, they felt France to be the injured party provoked by the Federalists anxious to serve monarchism above republicanism. Washington's farewell address was simply a Hamiltonian ploy to divert the nation from the real entangling connection, that of England. They cheered French victories on the Continent and toasted impending French invasions of England in 1795 and in 1797.[33]

Yet visceral support for the French cause against Britain and the surrogate Britons among the High Federalists did not signify any surrender to France or to the French Revolution under the Directory. Jeffersonian distress over the damage to France in the Jay Treaty was based on the threat of war, initiated by either the Directory or the Federalists. The alliance was the touchstone of the relationship. In 1795 and 1796, when news of that treaty spread through Europe and discredited Monroe, the American minister to Paris, they feared the French govenment's denunciation of the alliance would be a prelude to full scale war. Similarly in 1798, after France had humiliated the American commissioners sent by President Adams to Paris in the XYZ affair, they opposed the administration's unilateral abrogation of the alliance as a *casus belli*. Alliance in these

152

circumstances was a symbol of the status quo, not of American loyalty or even of gratitude.

While no specific information was available about France's imperial intentions in America, the treatment of European satellite nations did not go unnoticed even among partisans of France. The Directory's ambitions in Louisiana may not have been fully clear, but Madison had no hesitation about speculating on an angry France conspiring with the Spanish to disturb navigation on the Mississippi River.[34] Jefferson gloomily predicted that there will be "new neighbors in Louisiana (probably the present French armies when disbanded)," which he equated with "a combination of enemies on that side where we are most vulnerable."[35] And Monroe added an apocalyptic note by suggesting that if war should come, the Federalists would link America to England "as a feeble contemptible satellite." And if France wins, "we are then to experience that fate which she will then prescribe...."[36]

The Hamiltonians posed the most immediate danger of war by their exploitation of France's anger. Jefferson and his friends quickly saw that when Talleyrand, the French foreign minister, refused to deal with the American commissioners in 1798 until a suitable bribe had been offered, his mysterious emissaries, X, Y, and Z became a "dish cooked up" in such a way that the "swindlers are made to appear as the French government."[37] And even if the French foreign minister was a swindler, the insulting behavior was no cause of war. Madison railed against the "stupidity" rather than the depravity of Talleyrand. The Frenchman had lived a brief time in American exile, long enough in this country to know "the impossibility of secrecy."[38]

In the campaign for war against the Directory, the treaties of 1778 inevitably became the object of special attack. There was nothing new in this Hamiltonian assault. In 1792 the secretary of the treasury had proposed breaking off the alliance in return for British aid against the Spanish in New Orleans. A year later, after the Anglo-French war erupted, he urged the suspension of alliance on the grounds of its nullification by revolution.[39] But in 1793 he feared that the French connection would bring an American clash with Britain. In 1798 the severance had a different purpose; it was to launch a formal declaration of war against France, and with it, probably an alliance with England and suppression of Jeffersonian dissent.

Such was the scenario projected by the Jeffersonians in the summer of 1798. From the floor of the Congress, they worked against voiding the treaties. Albert Gallatin, a Jeffersonian leader from Pennsylvania in the House, admitted France's violations of the Treaty of Commerce, but claimed that the alliance was not affected by French measures. If the Federalists had asked for the voiding of the Treaty of Commerce, he could understand the argument, although he made it clear that Jay's Treaty with England would deserve denunciation along with the French Treaty. Additionally, he protested the "novel" nature of the proceedings, since there was no precedent for legislatures to repeal treaties.[40] This theme was developed at great length in the Philadelphia *General Advertiser,* where it was coupled with the state's rights thesis of government found in the Kentucky and Virginia Resolutions rejecting the Federalist Alien and Sedition laws of 1798. An editorial asked rhetorically: "is not every officer of a State Government sworn to uphold the Constitution of the United States? If the Federal Government passes laws contravening the Constitution, is it not a breach of oath in a state officer to carry such laws into effect?...If Congress can annul a contract with a foreign country because of its violation, will not the same justice operate to modifying or annulling a contract between states which is no longer regarded?"[41]

The debate over the alliance was all the more spirited because the French treaties were mixed with suppression of states' rights, as well as with Hamiltonian ambitions for alliance with Britain. But how much specific meaning did it have beyond its function as a weapon of internecine political combat? Were the Jeffersonians willing to risk war with Britain for the sake of either of the treaties of 1778? The answers were negative. A preliminary examination of the press in 1798, in search of occasions which would celebrate the alliance—such as the twentieth anniversary of its signing or of Independence Day— yields no affirmative position on the treaties. In fact, the anniversary went almost unnoticed on 6 February; the cheers of the democratic societies had vanished along with the societies themselves. Where toasts were raised to the day, as in Norfolk, "may it ever be distinguished," the purpose was no more than to urge "speedy accommodation of all differences between the two republics."[42] 4 July offered even less evidence of the commitment of 1778. Opposition to the annulment of the treaties was one thing; fulfillment of its obligation was quite another. When the word alliance was mentioned by the Rising Sun Militia Company of New York in its many toasts on Independence Day, it was against "all alliance with that almost ruined nation called Britain" and for friendship to all nations, "but in alliance with none."[43] No exception was made for the French alliance.

When it became apparent to Jeffersonians that the break between the Adams and the Hamiltonian Federalists was genuine and permanent and that the new mission to France intended seriously to reduce conflict and to repair the breach with the ally, none of the opposition leaders took this to mean a reinstatement of the alliance. Jefferson put it clearly to Gerry, just returned from France in January 1799: "I am for free commerce with all nations; political connection with none; & little or no diplomatic establishment. And I am not for linking ourselves by new treaties with the quarrels of Europe."[44] It is difficult to distinguish this sentiment from Washington's farewell address in 1796 or from President Jefferson's inaugural address in 1801.

Critics, over the years, have attributed such words of Jefferson, Madison, or Monroe to either a shrewd pitch for votes in the presidential campaign of 1800 or to the temporary shock over Napoleon Bonaparte's coup d'etat of 9 November 1799. That Bonapartism affected the Jeffersonian judgment of France is not in question. Madison deplored France's defection from civil authority and felt it "left America as the only Theatre on which true liberty can have a fair trial."[45] Jefferson ruminated about men-on-horseback and made the connection between Bonaparte and Hamilton. If he could accept the former, and not the latter, it was only because France was fit for nothing better. The Consulate reflected the French lack of "the habit of self-government."[46]

But the Jeffersonian estrangement from France was deeper than Bonapartism and older than the most recent coup. Suspicions of French intentions in Louisiana and elsewhere, doubts of French reliability in commercial relations, fear of American entanglement in French imperial projects, or even in the republican struggles for survival—all had characterized Republican attitudes toward France from the beginnings of the Federal Union and indeed from the moment the alliance had been made. Such emotions as were felt for France or such calculations as were made on the basis of friendship with France were largely functions of domestic disarray and consequent fears of British designs on the United States. When those concerns were allayed, even temporarily, the familiar postures were restored. There were some differences in 1800. While British malevolence was to remain more dangerous than its French counterpart until the end of the war of 1812, the old dream of France replacing England as an economic partner died, never to revive. In its place was a vision of autarchy that was to become the American System a generation later.

When the Adams peace commissioners signed a new treaty with France in 1800 that terminated the alliance, there was not a single protest from Jefferson, his colleagues, or from the press which supported the new President. If Jefferson called it a "bungling" treaty, it was because it failed to win compensation for damages done to American shipping and because it might be regarded with hostility by the British.[47] President Jefferson was not much moved by such American friends in France as Joel Barlow or Paine who praised a new maritime convention the French were supporting in favor of the liberal maritime rulings, which both countries had subscribed to in 1778.[48] Neutral rights had lost their luster, if only because they had failed to affect British seapower. Jefferson pointedly agreed with George Logan, a devoted Pennsylvania peace seeker, that the United States ought to join no confederacies, even when they pursued laudable goals of freeing the seas for neutral trade: "It ought to be the very first object of our pursuits to have nothing to do with the European interests and politics."[49] This is American isolationism.

## NOTES

1. "Isolationism" first appeared in print in 1922. See Mitford M. Mathews, ed., *A Dictionary of Americanisms on Historical Principles* (Chicago: Univ. of Chicago Press, 1951), 1: 891.

2. Felix Gilbert, *To the Farewell Address: Ideas of Early American Foreign Policy* (Princeton: Princeton Univ. Press, 1961), 46ff.

3. W. C. Ford et al., eds., *The Journals of the Continental Congress* (34 vols., Washington, D.C.: Government Printing Office, 1904-1937), III, 392.

4. John Adams to John Winthrop, 23 June 1776, in Edmund C. Burnett, ed., *Letters of Members of Continental Congress* (8 vols., Washington, D.C.: Carnegie Institution, 1921-1936), I, 502.

5. "Plan of Treaties," *Journals of the Continental Congress,* VI, 768-78.

6. Harrison et al., Committee of Secret Correspondence to the Commissioner at Paris, Baltimore, 30 December 1776, in Francis Wharton, ed., *Revolutionary Diplomatic Correspondence of the United States* (6 vols., Washington, D.C.: Government Printing Office, 1889), II, 240.

7. Silas Deane memoir to French foreign minister, 30 December 1776, in Archives du Ministère des Affaires Étrangères, correspondance politique (États-Unis), transcript in Library of Congress, I, no. 15.

8. Arthur Lee to Baron Schulenberg, 10 June 1777, *Revolutionary Diplomatic Correspondence,* II, 334.

9. David Hunter Miller, *Treaties and Other International Acts of the United States of America* (8 vols., Washington, D.C.: Government Printing Office, 1931), II, 39.

10. Committee to Commissioners, 4 May 1778, *Revolutionary Diplomatic Correspondence,* II, 569.

11. Miller, *Treaties and Other International Acts,* Article 2 of Treaty of Alliance, II, 36-37.

12. *Journals of the Continental Congress,* XX, 8 June and 11 June 1781, 615-17, 627-28.

13. Robert Morris to Benjamin Franklin, 5 December 1781, in Robert Morris Papers, Library of Congress.

14. Morris to Franklin, 1 July 1782, ibid.

15. John Jay to Robert Livingston, 3 April 1782, in Jay Papers, Library of Congress.

16. Harold C. Syrett et al., eds., *The Papers of Alexander Hamilton,* (19 vols., New York: Columbia Univ. Press, 1961-), III, 294-95. Hamilton's remarks on the Provisional Peace Treaty in the Continental Congress, Philadelphia, 19 March 1783.

17. Debates in the Congress of the Confederation, 19 March 1783, in Gaillard Hunt, ed., *Writings of James Madison* (9 vols., New York: G. P. Putnam's Sons, 1900-1910), I, 404-05.

18. Debates in the Congress of the Confederation, 12 March 1783, ibid., I, 406.

19. Motion on the Provisional Peace Treaty in the Continental Congress, 19 March 1783, in Syrett, *Papers of Hamilton,* III, 296-97.

20. Debates in the Congress of the Confederation, 9-10 January 1783, Hunt, *Writings of Madison,* I, 306-07.

21. Debates in the Congress of the Confederation, 13 January 1783, ibid., III, 309.

22. William Stinchcombe observes that "The French-American defensive alliance ended in fact when the news arrived of the termination of hostilities between France and Great Britain in March, 1783," *The American Revolution and the French Alliance* (Syracuse: Syracuse Univ. Press, 1969), p. 200.

23. Reports of Secretary Jay, respecting French and American consuls, 4 July 1786, in *The Diplomatic Correspondence of the United States of America from the Signing of the Definitive Treaty of Peace to the Adoption of the Constitution, March 4, 1789* (3 vols., Washington, 1837), I, 226-27. See discussion in S. F. Bemis, "John Jay," in Bemis, ed., *American Secretaries of State and Their Diplomacy* (10 vols., New York: A. A. Knopf, 1928), I, 258; and Dumas Malone, *Jefferson and the Rights of Man, Jefferson and His Time* (5 vols., Boston: Little, Brown, 1948-), II, 199-201.

24. Elbridge Gerry to Rufus King, 21 March 1785, Gerry Papers, Library of Congress.

25. Jefferson to William Short, 28 July 1791, in Paul L. Ford, ed., *The Writings of Thomas Jefferson* (10 vols., New York: G. P. Putnam's Sons, 1892-1899), V, 362-63.

26. See discussion in Charles M. Thomas, *American Neutrality in 1793: A Study in Cabinet Government* (New York: Columbia Univ. Press, 1931), pp. 46-47; Charles S. Hyneman, *The First American Neutrality: A Study of the American Understanding of Neutral Obligations during the Years 1792 to 1815* (Urbana: Univ. of Illinois Press, 1934), pp. 12-13.

27. Jefferson to Gouvernor Morris, 12 March 1793, in Ford, *Writings of Jefferson,* VI, 199.

28. Letters of Helvidius, No. 3, in Hunt, *Writings of James Madison,* VI, 167.

29. Monroe to Jefferson, 3 September 1793, in S. M. Hamilton, *The Writings of James Monroe,* (7 vols., New York: G. P. Putnam's Sons, 1898-1903), I, 274.

30. Eugene P. Link, *Democratic-Republican Societies, 1790-1800* (New York: Columbia Univ. Press, 1942), p. 20. Identifies them with

Sons of Liberty and contemporary British radical clubs.

31. Jefferson to Madison, 28 April 1793, in Ford, *Writings of Jefferson,* VI, 232.

32. Jefferson to Edmond Genêt, 17 June 1793, in A. Lipscomb, *The Writings of Thomas Jefferson* (20 vols., Washington, D.C.: Thomas Jefferson Memorial Association, 1904), IX, 131-37.

33. Jefferson to W. B. Giles, 27 April 1795, in Ford, *Writings of Jefferson,* VIII, 172. Particularly noteworthy was Jefferson's impulse to give up his retirement in 1795 to dine in London with General Pichegru and to "hail the dawn of liberty & republicanism in that island."

34. Madison to Jefferson, 25 December 1796; to Colonel James Madison, 27 November 1796, in Madison Papers, Library of Congress.

35. Jefferson to Thomas Pinckney, 29 May 1797, Lipscomb and Bergh, *Writings of Jefferson,* IX, 389-90.

36. Monroe to Jefferson, 16 June 1798, *Writings of Monroe,* III, 126.

37. Jefferson to Edmund Pendleton, 29 January 1799, in Ford, *Writings of Jefferson,* VII, 337.

38. Madison to Jefferson, 15 April 1798, in Hunt, *Writings of Madison,* VI, 315.

39. Jefferson's Anas, 31 October 1792, in Ford, *Writings of Jefferson,* I, 207. Unpublished article for the *Gazette of the United States,* March-April 1793, in Syrett, *Papers of Hamilton,* XIV, 268.

40. *Annals of Congress,* 5th Cong., 2nd Sess., H.R., 6 July 1798, 2126.

41. Philadelphia General Advertiser, 12 July 1798.

42. Ibid., 26 February 1798.

43. Ibid., 10 July 1798.

44. Jefferson to Gerry, 26 January 1799, in Ford, *Writings of Jefferson,* VII, 328.

45. Madison to Jefferson, 24 April 1800, in Hunt, *Writings of Madison,* VI, 408.

46. Jefferson to John Breckinridge, 29 January 1800, in Ford, *Writings of Jefferson,* VII, 417-18.

47. Jefferson to Madison, 19 December 1800, in Lipscomb and Bergh, *Writings* X, 185.

48. Paine to Jefferson, 1 October and 4 October 1800, Jefferson Papers, Library of Congress; Barlow to Jefferson, 3 October 1800, ibid. Many of Paine's views were made public in extracts of his letters written in October 1800 and appear in the *National Intellegencer,* 26 January and 11 February 1801.

49. Jefferson to Logan, 21 March 1801, in Ford, *Writings of Jefferson,* VIII, 23.

# INDEX

Adams, John, 45, 47-51, 53-60, 70, 74, 75, 77-81, 113, 115, 118-20, 139-41, 156; on balance of power, 54, 56, 58-59; on balance of trade, 55; distrust of French and Spanish monarchies, 57; on international commerce, 48; and Model Treaty, 43, 69, 137; and Montesquieu, 78; philosophes, influence on, 43; as President, 152

Adams, John Quincy, 79

Adams Federalists, 155

Alien and Sedition Acts, 154

American commerce, 23, 46-50, 74, 140, 146, 157; Mediterranean shipping, 146; statist economy of, 52; trade with French West Indies, 140, 146

American foriegn policy, 29, 40-50, 53, 54, 56-62, 70, 72-75, 77, 81, 111-17, 119, 125, 134-39, 148-58; alliance with Britain, 155; Anglo-Emerican relations, 14, 17, 18, 155; conciliatory plan for England, 17; effect of philosophes on, 41-48, 76-77; isolationism, 40-49, 75, 134-35, 157-58; neutrality, 112, 114, 115, 148-49, 150-51, 157; neutrality in Anglo-French War, 151; Progressive nature of, 41-42, 61; relations with Denmark, 121-24; relations with France, 29-32, 46, 71-75, 115-18, 125-26, 134-38, 140,

141, 147-56; relations with Great Britain, 2, 17, 20-23, 29, 57-61, 87, 91, 95, 121-22, 126, 143, 146, 149; relations with the Netherlands, 113-22; relations with Portugal, 121-24; relations with Russia, 89; relations with Spain, 73; relations with Sweden, 121; treaty with France, 29, 30, 32, 71, 73-75, 115, 125, 126, 135, 138, 146, 147, 149-51, 154-56; treaty with Prussia, 121, 122, 124, 125, 127; treaty with Spain, 73

American System, 156

American territorial claims, 136

American Treaty, Plan of 1776, 113, 115, 118, 131, 137

Anglican Church, 91

Anglo-American treaty, 126

Anglo-Dutch Treaty of 1674, 113-14

Anglo-French crisis, 148

Anglo-French war, 151, 154

Anglo-Russian treaties: of 1734, 114, 118; of 1766, 114, 117, 123

Armed Neutrality, 114-20, 123, 125, 126; Declaration of, 121-23

Articles of Confederation, 69, 141, 145, 147

Balance of power, 56, 58, 59, 61, 62, 73, 81, 87, 126, 139; European, 53-55, 62, 70, 76

161

163

# CONTRIBUTORS

Alan S. Brown, Ph.D., Michigan, 1953, is professor of history at Western Michigan University. Among his publications are "The British Peace Officer of 1778," *Papers* of the Michigan Academy of Science, Arts, and Letters, 40 (1955), and "The Role of the Army in Western Settlement: Josiah Harmar's Command, 1785-1790," *Pennsylvania Magazine of History and Biography* (1969). He is currently doing research for a biography of John G. Simcoe, Lieutenant Governor of Canada from 1791 to 1795.

Carl B. Cone, Ph.D., Iowa, 1940, has been a member of the History Department of the University of Kentucky since 1947. He is the author of many works in eighteenth-century British history, most notably his two-volume study, *Torchbearer of Freedom: Burke and the Nature of Freedom* (1957 & 1964) and *The English Jacobins* (1968). He has recently completed a biography of George III.

David M. Griffiths, Ph.D., Cornell, 1967, is associate professor of Russian History at the University of North Carolina at Chapel Hill. With an M.A. Columbia, 1964, in American history he has specialized in Russian-American relations during the American Revolution, published in his findings in the *Slavic Review* and *Russian Review* as well as in the *William and Mary Quarterly*. He is preparing a large-scale study of Russian-American relations in the late eighteenth century.

James H. Hutson, Ph.D. Yale, 1964, is presently Coordinator of the American Revolution Bicentennial Office, Library of Congress and former member of the Yale faculty. Author of *Pennsylvania Politics, 1746-1770* (1972) and co-editor, *Essays on the American Revolution* (1973), he was earlier Editor of Publications, Institute of Early American History and Culture, Williamsburg. He has recently finished a manuscript on John Adams.

Lawrence S. Kaplan, Ph.D. Yale, 1951, has been a member of the Kent State University History Department since 1954. His works include *Jefferson and France* (1967), *Colonies into Nation: American Diplomacy, 1763-1801* (1972), and a forthcoming book of essays (with Morrell Heald) on *Culture and Diplomacy: the American Experience.*

Gregg L. Lint, Ph.D. Michigan State, 1975, is assistant editor of the Papers of John Adams at the Massachusetts Historical Society, a project of the Belknap Press of Harvard University Press at the Massachusetts Historical Society. He is additionally undertaking a study of the law of nations and American foreign policy between 1776 and 1815.

William C. Stinchcombe, Ph.D., Michigan, 1967 is associate professor of History at Syracuse University and diplomatic editor of the Papers of John Marshall. His publications include *The French Alliance and the American Revolution* (1969) and "Talleyrand and the American Negotiations of 1797-1798," *Journal of American History* (1975). He is currently engaged in editing the papers of John Marshall's mission to Paris.